John Lyons'

Bringing Up Baby

FROM **HORSE &RIDER**

20 Progressive Ground-Work Exercises
to Develop Your **Young Horse** Into a
Reliable, Accepting Partner

BY JOHN LYONS WITH JENNIFER J. DENISON

JOHN LYONS' BRINGING UP BABY
by John Lyons with Jennifer J. Denison

PRIMEDIA Enthusiast Group

Copyright © 2002 PRIMEDIA Enthusiast Publications,
d.b.a. PRIMEDIA Equine Network
656 Quince Orchard Road, #600
Gaithersburg, MD 20878
301-977-3900

Order by calling 800-952-5813 or online at **www.theequinecollection.com**

Printed in the USA.

Author: John Lyons
Editor: Jennifer Denison
Art Director: Lauryl Suire Eddlemon
Photographer: Darrell Dodds
Production and Marketing: Julie Beaulieu

The author and publisher shall have neither liability nor responsibility to any person or entity with respect to any loss or damage caused or alleged to be caused directly or indirectly by the information contained in this book. While the book is as accurate as the author can make it, there may be errors, omissions, or inaccuracies.

Library of Congress Cataloging-in-Publication Data

Lyons, John, 1947-
  [Bringing up baby]
  John Lyons' bringing up baby : 20 progressive ground-work exercises to
develop your young horse into a reliable, accepting partner / by John
Lyons with Jennifer J. Denison.
    p. cm.
  ISBN 1-929164-12-2
  1. Horses--Training. 2. Human-animal communication. I. Title:
Bringing up baby. II. Denison, Jennifer J., 1973- III. Title.
  SF287 .L955 2002
  636.1'088--dc21
                        2002001208

CONTENTS

Before you begin training, review these tips to ensure
safe, successful, stress-free lessons for you and your
youngster.

Use this round-pen exercise to teach your weanling to
turn and face you on cue—then stand there quietly—so
you can safely approach him.

Introduce your youngster to unfamiliar objects, while
instilling trust and confidence, with this simple sack-out
method.

Safely restrain your weanling with a halter, using this
gentle haltering technique.

Add direction to your ground-work sessions—and teach
your youngster to longe—with this force-free leading
lesson.

Use rope work to accustom your weanling to hind-leg
stimuli, and to lay a foundation for handling his hind feet.

Bathe your youngster—without creating a water fight—
using this no-stress technique.

Teach your weanling to accept clipping with this gradual,
common-sense approach.

Gain control of your youngster's movement by isolating
and directing individual body parts, using this pressure-
release maneuver.

Build on your foundation of control by practicing this
longe-line routine.

Reprogram your weanling's "catch me if you can" attitude by teaching him to come to you on command.

Enhance communication with your youngster—and
refine his responsiveness to body language—with this
pressure-free leading lesson.

Use this pressure-release, tie-training technique to encourage your weanling to accept restraint without pulling back.

Teach your youngster to cross three common trail obstacles in-hand to develop his confidence and coordination.

Make trailer loading and unloading trouble-free with
this progressive enter-and-exit process.

Make hoof-handling hassle-free with this step-by-step
sequence.

Prepare your youngster for the bitting and bridling process by performing these four simple head-down drills.

Build on the previous lesson's skills by introducing your
young horse to a snaffle bit and bridle.

Use this proven seven-step suppling system to increase
your youngster's flexibility and responsiveness to direct-
rein pressure.

Encourage your young horse to move his hips away from
you in response to rein pressure to gain control of his
hindquarters.

Gradually introduce your youngster to the saddle to prepare him for his first ride, with this stress-free saddling
process.

INTRODUCTION

At my clinics and symposiums, and through correspondence, I hear from hundreds of horsepeople like you each week, asking for advice on training young horses. Specifically, how to lay a strong foundation for a youngster, so he won't develop bad habits—including head shyness and spookiness—that may come back to haunt future under-saddle endeavors. Now, I'll give you my proven, step-by-step program for developing your youngster into a trusting, tractable partner. In this 20-lesson workbook, you'll perform a series of ground-work exercises—from teaching your youngster to turn and face you as you approach him, to loading in the trailer, to standing still for the saddle. You'll use gradual persuasion—rather than force—to build a strong foundation of trust and confidence for a lasting partnership between you and your young horse, whether his future lies in or out of the show ring.

—John Lyons

ACKNOWLEDGMENTS

Special thanks to:

• The editors and contributing editors at *Horse & Rider*—Sue M. Copeland, Jennifer Forsberg Meyer, Marilee Bond Nudo, and René E. Riley—for their editorial guidance.

• Darrell Dodds, Editor, *Paint Horse Journal*, for his never-ending patience during photo shoots, and for capturing John's methods so clearly on film.

• Monica Smith of Rifle, Colorado, for allowing us to use the Paint Horse weanling, True Queen Bee, as our equine model in the "Weanling Training" section of this book.

• Kenneth and Jennifer Banks of Banks Quarter Horse Ranch in Schulenburg, Texas, for allowing us to use the Quarter Horse colt, Star Potential, as our equine model in "The Yearling Year" section of this book. Also, for allowing us to use their beautiful facility for our photo shoot.

ABOUT THE AUTHORS

JOHN LYONS

John Lyons, known as "America's most trusted trainer," is renowned for his gentle, conditioned-response training approach. Through his 20-plus years of conducting clinics, demonstrations, and symposiums, and his extensive collection of books and videos, he has helped thousands of horse owners worldwide increase their understanding of their horses, and achieve a trusting relationship with them. The hallmark of John's training style is his use of gradual, step-by-step lesson plans to teach a horse to do just about anything. According to John, breaking a skill down into many simple steps sets a horse up for success by gradually building his confidence and increasing his understanding of what's being asked of him.

In 1995, John's methods were put to the test when his beloved Appaloosa stallion, Bright Zip, lost his eyesight due to an allergic reaction to a vaccine. With patience and perseverance, though, the duo developed an even stronger bond, and gradually adjusted to Zip's blindness. Today, Zip is a regular attraction at equine-related events across the country.

John resides at his Cowboy Up Ranch in Parachute, Colorado. He has four grown children—daughters Tammy Jo Lewis, Sandy Nickal, and Brandi DeVoto, and son Josh—and seven grandchildren. Josh is following in his father's bootsteps, conducting clinics and overseeing the 12-week certification programs. For more information on John Lyons, write to P.O. Box 479, Parachute, CO 81635, call (970)285-9797, or log on to **www.johnlyons.com**.

JENNIFER J. DENISON

Jennifer began her equine-journalism career at *Horse & Rider* more than 6 years ago, as a college intern. She's since worked her way up to senior editor. When she's not writing about horses for the magazine, the life-long horsewoman enjoys trail riding and competing in Western events, especially barrel racing and pole bending. She and her husband, Robert, live with their horses outside of Woodland Park, Colorado.

Jennifer's two instructional training series with John Lyons, *Bringing Up Baby* (*Horse & Rider*, January '99 through February '00) and *The Yearling Year* (*Horse & Rider*, July '00 to December '00), both featured in this guide, earned her coveted first-place honors from American Horse Publications.

SAFETY GUIDELINES

Keep these pointers in mind during all sessions to help make learning safe, fun, and stress-free for both you and your youngster.

• *Initially, perform all lessons in the same 50- to 60-foot round pen (or similar enclosure).* A round work area enables you to safely drive your youngster forward without losing control. The familiar environment will also help keep him relaxed and attuned to your cues. Once he's mastered a particular lesson, you can further hone that skill in new surroundings. (*Tip:* Avoid a square or rectangular area, such as a paddock. Its corners could confuse your weanling and entrap him, increasing the likelihood of him running through the fence. If you only have such an area, "round" or block the corners by attaching boards across them.)

• *Keep your lessons simple.* The more you can break down a lesson into its component parts, the easier and faster your youngster will learn—and retain—the skill you've taught him. That's because he'll have simple cornerstones to build upon until he achieves the final goal. (If you discover a technique that helps communicate a particular concept to your weanling better than the one I've explained, use it.)

• *Handle with care.* If your weanling is fresh, he may be prone to kick, buck, or strike out until you've worked the edge off him. He'll also be unable to focus on the lesson. This is especially true if he's housed in a stall or small paddock, so develops pent-up energy. If he's fresh (you'll know because he'll be reactive, and will move with his head, neck, and tail tense, above their normal positions), work him quietly around the pen until he settles, staying out of striking/kicking range (see below). You'll know he's ready to focus on the lesson when his head and tail consistently assume their normal, relaxed position.

• *Stay out of kicking range.* In the beginning, it's a good idea to position yourself at least 12 feet from your youngster's hindquarters to avoid getting kicked. As he gets comfortable with you working around him and handling his hind legs, you can gradually work your way closer to him. But never stand directly behind him, where you'd be an easy target; instead, stand opposite his shoulder or hip.

• *Review previous lessons.* Before you begin a new lesson, make sure your weanling reliably performs the previous ones. You can't expect him to learn a more advanced maneuver until he completely understands the foundation exercises.

• *Avoid tying your youngster initially.* Until he learns this advanced form of restraint (see "Lesson 12: Tie-Training" on page 57), he could seriously injure himself if he were to be tied and pull back. He could also develop a dangerous habit you want to avoid instilling.

• *Monitor your weanling's comfort level.* To avoid injury to either of you, make sure your youngster is relaxed and comfortable with his surroundings and your presence. You'll know he's accepting the situation when he's holding his head and neck at a natural level, relaxing his body, and investigating his environment by sniffing around or nibbling grass. Watch for signs of nervousness, which include: pinned ears, an elevated head and neck, a tensed body, and a raised leg. If you notice any of these signposts, or ever feel you or him are at risk for injury, stop what you're doing. Then return to a point in the lesson (or a previous lesson) where you're both comfortable, and slowly begin again.

• *Use concise, consistent cues.* The more clearly you communicate with your weanling, the less likely he'll become confused, and the more quickly he'll learn. If he doesn't respond correctly right away, that's okay; repeat the same cueing sequence until he performs the desired response.

• *Progress patiently.* Avoid proceeding to the next step (or next lesson) until your youngster has mastered the previous one. It may take a few minutes or a few sessions before he'll consistently respond to your cues. Impatient handling now will come back to haunt you in the future, in the form of resistance.

• *Avoid overdoing it.* Young horses learn at different speeds. For best results, limit your training sessions to a maximum of 30 minutes, two to three times per week, to avoid tiring your weanling physically and mentally. Also, his bones are still developing and are easily stressed with hard work, so avoid circling him more than four times during round-pen exercises without allowing him a moment to rest. This is especially important if you're working on deep or hard ground, where his legs will tire quickly.

• *Move slowly.* Quick, sudden movements could startle your youngster, causing him to tense up, run away, kick at you, or learn to fear your presence—all the opposite of your goal.

• *Avoid chasing your weanling.* Doing so could cause him to fear your approach. If he turns and runs in response to a particular step, ask him to stop, then turn and face you. (See "Lesson 1: Turn & Face" on page 10.) When he's relaxed, slowly begin again.

• *Forget force.* In exercises requiring the use of a lead rope, lariat, or longe line, avoid jerking or pulling on the line. Using strength to reprimand your youngster will only teach him to brace against pressure and fear your presence.

• *Render frequent rewards.* Whenever your weanling responds correctly to your cues—or improves his response—immediately reward him with rubs, encouraging words, and a moment of relaxation. This conditioned-response technique will gradually build his confidence and skills.

• *Always end on a good note.* Find a place at which your youngster is relaxed and confident before ending a lesson—even if it means going back to an earlier lesson. Doing so will build his confidence and keep him willing to learn.

WEANLING TRAINING

Turn & Face

Learn how to safely approach your weanling by gaining his attention—and respect—with this round-pen exercise.

In this lesson, you'll learn how to safely approach your youngster by teaching him to turn and face you on cue, then stand quietly. By teaching him this skill, you'll gain three important benefits: 1) You'll avoid such dangerous problems as having him crowd or push into you when led, because you'll teach him not to evade your space; 2) you'll reduce the risk of getting kicked when you enter his stall, paddock, or pasture; and 3) you'll be a step ahead for future lessons in which you'll be asking him to stand quietly while you work around him.

You'll use my round-pen method, which is designed to help you gain control of your weanling's mind and body. You'll first learn how to use body language to direct his movement around the pen. By maneuvering him in this manner, he'll come to respect—and not intrude upon—your space (the area surrounding your body). Then you'll teach him to turn, face, and focus both eyes on you, using a kiss cue.

Before you begin, review the "Safety Guidelines" on page 6, to help make your round-pen sessions safe, successful, and stress-free for you and your youngster.

You'll need:
• A dressage whip or lariat.

1. Herd your weanling into the round pen, or have him follow a pasturemate into it, and close the gate. (Once your youngster is inside the pen, remove the other horse.) Begin your lesson by slowly approaching your weanling. If he hasn't had much previous handling, his reaction is likely to resemble that of this filly's. That is, his "fight or flight" instincts will be triggered by your approach, causing him to tense up (note this filly's raised head and stiff body) and turn tail on you (a sign that he's ready, willing, and able to kick!), as he seeks an escape route. If he reacts in this manner, slow your approach, or stop until he relaxes. Otherwise, continuing toward him could cause him to kick or run through the fence. On the other hand, if he has been handled and/or remains relaxed as you walk toward him...

2. ...proceed to move him around the pen in the direction you want him to go. (I'll explain how to move your youngster on a circle to the left; simply reverse these instructions for a circle to the right.) Step toward your weanling's left (inside) hip, but not within kicking range. If he doesn't immediately move away, raise your dressage whip or lariat toward his left hip. He should move off to the left at a walk or trot. If he lopes, step across the pen toward the front of his nose, to "block" his motion.

(The lope will place a lot of concussion on your youngster's legs, which could induce lameness. Plus, loping may tire him more quickly than the slower gaits.)

As your weanling circles the pen, continue to drive him forward by walking a smaller inner circle, keeping your body positioned behind his hip. If he tries to change direction on his own, step firmly toward the front of his nose to block his turn, then step toward his inside hip once more to guide him back on the original circle. Keep him moving in the same direction, until he'll do so without trying to turn and go the opposite way. When he's moving consistently in that direction...

3. ...ask him to reverse direction (in this case, move on a circle to the right). Briskly step toward a point on the fence that's about 20 feet in front of your youngster's nose, forming a barrier to reverse his motion.

Avoid crowding your weanling too quickly or too closely to the fence, because he could become nervous and run into it. If it appears he might hit the fence, or if he tries to run over you, step back to the center of the pen and let him go by. That way, neither of you gets hurt. As soon as he passes by, quickly walk to the same spot at the fence where you initially asked him to change direction, and stand there quietly. He's likely to reverse direction on the opposite side of the round pen to avoid the physical barrier you've created.

4. When your youngster turns to the right, step toward his right (inside) hip to send him forward in the new direction. As soon as he takes off, step back to release your pressure, then reward him with kind words. Repeat the reverse-and-go-forward exercise in both directions, until he'll instantly change direction in response to your body lanuage; he'll immediately move off when you step toward his hip; and he'll consistently go in the direction you're asking without reversing on his own. It may take several sessions to accomplish this.

5. Next, use these turning points to teach your weanling to stop and face you on cue. Gradually decrease the distance between direction changes to about every 10 to 12 feet. Here's how it works: Your youngster naturally slows down to reverse direction. By shortening the distance—and thus the frequency—between changes, he'll begin to turn more slowly than he has been. Eventually, he'll stop between changes. (You can also reinforce your stop message with the verbal cue "whoa.")

Begin by moving your weanling around the pen in the direction you specify. After he travels 10 feet, ask him to reverse direction. Repeat this turning process in both directions, until he stops during the turn, as this filly has.

When he stops, step back toward the pen's center to release your pressure, as I'm demonstrating, and reward him with kind words. Also, allow him to stand and relax for a moment, so he knows he's responded correctly and can feel secure with you inside the pen.

6. Now you're ready to get your youngster in position to turn and face you, and follow you with his eyes. If he stopped with his head facing the fence, reposition him so he's standing parallel to it. To get him to face left (reverse these cues to get him to face right), ask him to walk in that direction by stepping toward his left (inside) hip. Then immediately step toward his nose, as though you're asking him to reverse direction. This time, however, discontinue your movement before he changes direction, allowing him to stop when he's parallel to the fence, facing left. If he turns away from you, repeat this step-and-stop maneuver until he stands still, parallel to the fence, facing left. Then reward him. (Note this filly is already looking at me. This is the response you're after.)

Next, walk 15 feet in front of your weanling, and stand beside the fence. This puts you in a spot where he can easily focus on you. Stand there for several minutes, until he's comfortable with your close proximity. If he begins to back up or turn away, quickly step around toward his nose, asking him to turn back and stand parallel to the fence again, facing left.

When your youngster is in proper position, encourage him to turn and look at you with both eyes, as this filly has, by making a kissing noise, or tapping a dressage whip or lariat against your leg for attention-attracting movement.

7. If your weanling doesn't turn and look at you within 2 seconds, step toward the center of the round pen, drive him forward three to four steps, and repeat Steps 5 and 6. With consistent practice, he'll learn to look at you whenever he hears the kiss cue.

This filly has responded not only by turning and facing me, but also by walking toward me. If your youngster does this, reward him. If he doesn't, that's okay; you'll work up to this advanced maneuver in a future lesson. (See "Lesson 10: Come On Cue" on page 49.)

8. Now, ask your weanling to focus his gaze on you even when you move away from him. To do so, first walk toward him, stopping just before the point you think he'll step away. Then take one or two steps back toward the center of the pen. If he looks away from you, kiss and/or tap your whip or rope to get his attention. If he moves off, repeat Steps 5 through 8, until he'll remain still and focused on you.

Continue this walk-stop-move-away sequence, gradually stepping closer to your youngster, then farther away from him, making him look at

you for a longer duration. With practice, he'll turn and face you, and follow you with his eyes no matter where you go in the pen. This is the start of a trusting and respectful partnership that you'll build on in the remaining lessons.

SACKING OUT

In this lesson, you'll learn how to sack out your youngster—that is, to rub different objects all over his body as a way to accustom him to the feel, sight, and sound of scary stimuli. By building his confidence with this exercise, you'll teach him to control his natural flight-or-fight instincts in response to something new. This work will also develop his trust in you, and help prevent such annoying—and potentially dangerous—problems as head-shyness, kicking, and spookiness.

Help control your weanling's natural flight-or-fight reaction with this simple sack-out technique.

You'll begin by slowly rubbing your weanling with the least intimidating object in your collection, your hand. Once he accepts that, you'll progress to rubbing him with scarier ones.

Follow these tips, as well as the "Safety Guidelines" on page 6, to help guarantee safe, successful, stress-free sack-out sessions for you and your youngster.

• *Work in the center of the pen.* That way, you'll help avoid getting trapped between your youngster and the fence if he should become frightened. To get him to the center of the pen, ask him to circle left (or right if you prefer, as long as it's the direction *you* want him to go) by stepping toward his inside hip. After he's taken a few steps, walk in front of him to stop his motion. Then kiss to him to get him to turn and look at you.

• *Sack out both sides of your weanling equally.* This will make him less likely to spook when you walk around him or approach him from the *off* (right) side.

• *Avoid tying your youngster.* You haven't introduced him to this advanced skill yet (but will do so in "Lesson 12: Tie Training" on page 57), so risk his pulling back and getting injured. This training error also reinforces the message that it's okay to pull back while standing tied—a statement you want to avoid instilling.

You'll need:

• At least 50 different barn items, ranging in size, texture, and degree of intimidation. (Some of the items I've selected include—in order from the least intimidating to most daunting: a rag, grooming mitt, brush, leg boot, lariat, halter, Navajo blanket, saddle pad, sandwich bag, garbage bag, slicker, and saddle cover. I'll only use a few items in this lesson for simplicity. However, the more items you expose your youngster to, the more practice he'll have at controlling his flight instincts.)

1. Herd your weanling into the round pen or have him follow a pasturemate into it, then remove the other horse, and close the gate. When your youngster is settled, use the kiss cue you taught him in the previous lesson to get him to turn and face you. When he does so, you're ready to sack him out with your hand—the least aggressive and intimidating approach.

Begin by getting your youngster to look at you, as you did in the previous lesson. When you have his attention, slowly reach out and gently touch his forehead with your hand. (It may take one or several sessions to do so.) Then advance to slowly rubbing it. If he remains relaxed, as this filly has, (note her natural head and neck position, and swiveled-forward ears), continue your slow rubbing motion, gradually working up to his left ear, down the left side of his neck, then back to his forehead. If he tenses up, immediately back away to release your pressure before he moves off. If he escapes, your natural tendency will probably be to grab and try to hold him. Such a quick approach could scare him, and ultimately cause him to run into the fence or kick out. Instead, kiss to him, signaling him to turn and face you. Then slowly begin again.

2. When your weanling is comfortable having both his shoulders rubbed, work down his left front leg. To safely do this, position yourself opposite his muzzle, facing his hindquarters. Bending at the waist, rub down his leg, while keeping your head away from his hind leg. Rotate rubbing his head, ears, neck, shoulders, and front leg, until he's completely relaxed with your touch. Then continue down that leg in the same gradual manner, until you reach his foot. Be sure to repeat on the opposite leg.

3. Once you can rub your weanling's entire front end on both sides without him tensing up or moving away, gradually work your way back to his hindquarters, using the approach outlined in Steps 1 and 2. Slowly rub along his back, and down his hips and hind legs. Stand in front of his hind legs and close to his body (to avoid getting kicked), until he's completely comfortable having his hind legs handled.

If your youngster's demeanor resembles this filly's (raised head and neck, and pinned ears, indicating she's nervous), make your movements extra slow. When he's comfortable, repeat this sack-out process with a pair of gloves on. Then build up to such items as a rag, towel, soft brush, and splint boot.

4. Next, sack out your weanling with a lariat, using the same gradual front-to-back process. (*Tip:* Keep your lariat coiled at first, so it's not as intimidating to your youngster as it'd be uncoiled. When he accepts it, you can practice with it uncoiled.)

This filly's head and neck are raised, but she's simply resting her head on my shoulder, which tells me she's relaxed. Before you move to Step 5, expose your weanling to several more items, until he readily accepts them. (I suggest a Navajo blanket, slicker, and canvas saddle cover.)

5. You're now ready to introduce one of the largest, heaviest, and thus most intimidating objects in your collection, the saddle pad. It's one you ultimately want to get on your youngster's back in preparation for his future under-saddle training. To start, approach him with the saddle pad, and allow him to smell and look at it.

Notice that this filly is concerned about the pad (indicated by her raised head, stiff neck, and wide eyes). If your weanling's reaction is similar, continue to let him examine the pad until he's comfortable. When he lowers his head and relaxes his muscles, proceed to the next step.

6. Rub the pad along your youngster's head, ears, neck, shoulders, and front legs, as you did with the other objects.

7. As your weanling becomes comfortable with the pad's sensation (you'll know he has when he remains relaxed as you rub him with it), slide it over his neck and on his back. If he appears nervous, return to rubbing him with the pad, gradually working up to sliding it on his back. Once he remains relaxed, slide the pad across his back and tap it with your hands, simulating the feel of a saddle being put on him. Then repeat this slide-and-tap routine, until you can simply lay the pad on his back without him becoming nervous or moving away. Notice that this filly is relaxed, as she's ignoring the pad and eating grass. Such acceptance is your goal.

8. As an introduction to the next two lessons on haltering and leading, respectively, you'll finish this sack-out session with a halter and lead rope. Introduce these objects one at a time, using the gentle technique you've learned in this lesson.

HALTERING

You're ready to halter your youngster for the first time. My gentle haltering method will enable you to safely catch and restrain him for grooming and other ground work, without him becoming nervous at the sight of a halter and lead rope. You'll begin where you left off in the previous lesson, sacking him out with the halter and lead rope. Then you'll gradually slip the halter over his nose and buckle it. You'll finish by removing the halter.

Teach your weanling the foundation of restraint with this gentle haltering approach.

You'll need:
• A well-fitting halter. (It's often difficult to find a store-bought halter that will properly fit a growing youngster. You may need to punch holes in the halter, as I have, for a snug fit.) I like leather or nylon halters, because they distribute pressure over a wide area, as opposed to rope halters, which apply pressure to narrow areas, creating pain for your weanling.

1. Herd your youngster into the round pen or have him follow a pasturemate into it, then remove the other horse, and close the gate. When your weanling is settled, ask him to turn and face you, then rub the halter and lead rope all over his body using the sack-out technique you learned in the previous lesson. In the beginning stages of this haltering process, your goal is simply to make him comfortable with the gear being near his head. This introductory work will make it easy to put on the halter, because he won't fear it. As he accepts the halter and lead rope, introduce him to the sensation of having them on top of his head by draping them over one ear, as shown. When he's comfortable with the items dangling on that ear, repeat this procedure on his other side, then drape it over both ears.

This filly appears comfortable, as evidenced by her level head and neck position, and relaxed expression. If your youngster remains relaxed, reward him by rubbing his forehead and telling him he's doing well. If he tenses up and raises his head and neck, slowly remove the tack. Then try again. If he moves away, avoid trying to grab or chase him. Such an aggressive approach could cause him to panic. Instead, allow him to settle. Then ask him to turn and face you, and begin again.

2. Once your weanling will stand quietly with the tack draped across both ears, introduce him to the feel of the halter sliding on and off his nose. (First, remove the lead rope so it doesn't become entangled and interfere with the haltering process.) Stand on his left side and hold the halter below his nose, allowing him to smell and investigate it. (If your youngster nibbles on the halter, that's okay. It shows acceptance.) When he accepts the dangling halter, hold its buckle in your left hand, and slowly reach your right arm over his neck to grasp the halter's crownpiece. Gradually slide the halter on and off his nose 10 to 15 times, inching it farther up his nose each repetition. If he objects to this by tensing up or raising his head and neck, remove the halter. Then slowly try again. If he moves away, use your kiss cue to signal him to stop and look at you. Then repeat this step. Continue this on-off routine until he relaxes and accepts the halter's feel.

Next, advance by teaching your weanling to move his nose toward the halter. To do so, stand on his left side and hold the halter just below his nose, as shown. Kiss to him to gain his attention; as he turns his head to look at you, he'll also move his nose toward the halter. Praise him with encouragement when he does. With repetition, he'll learn to flex his neck toward you and move his nose toward the halter, as this filly has.

3. Now, slowly slip the halter on, pulling the crownpiece over your youngster's poll and buckling it. If he tenses up or raises his head and neck, repeat Step 2. This filly has lowered her head and neck, and isn't paying attention to the halter, indicating she's accepted the sensation.

When your weanling will stand relaxed with the halter on for a few minutes, remove it by unbuckling the strap and slowly sliding it off his nose. If he starts to move away from you, immediately cue him to turn and face you. Otherwise, he'll learn to associate the halter's removal with pulling away from you—a dangerous habit. Repeat this on-off sequence, gradually allowing him to stand with the halter on for a longer duration, until he remains relaxed while you put it on and take it off. When you can consistently halter him without him becoming nervous, he's ready for my leading lesson.

LEADING

Add direction to your weanling's ground work—and introduce him to longeing—with this progressive leading lesson.

Y ou've haltered your youngster for the first time, introducing him to restraint. Now you'll build on that session by training him to lead willingly. By teaching him this important lesson, you'll also introduce him to three key skills: yielding to pressure, responding to body language, and longeing. All three elements will improve the communication between you and him that will become paramount in future lessons and under-saddle work.

You'll fasten a lariat or longe line to your weanling's halter. Then, at a standstill, you'll teach him to bend his head and neck when you exert gentle sideways pressure on the line.

When he'll consistently bend with light contact, you'll use my longeing exercise to teach him to yield to pressure while moving, as he'll be required to do when you lead him.

You'll gradually remove slack from the line as he yields to the pressure, until you're walking opposite his shoulder. With practice, he'll learn to move in response to your body movements, rather than to pressure. This will ultimately keep him light—that is, controllable with minimal contact.

You'll need:

- A well-fitting halter.
- A soft, cotton lead rope.
- A lariat.

1. Herd your weanling into a round pen or have him follow a pasturemate into it, then remove the other horse, and close the gate. When your youngster is relaxed, slip a halter on him, using the technique outlined in the previous lesson. If he remains quiet, you're ready to progress. But if he appears nervous, return to the previous lesson.

Next, attach a lariat to the halter ring below your weanling's chin. To fasten the lariat, take apart its loop, so you have one continuous length of rope with the *honda* (an eyelet that you feed slack through to form the loop) at one end. Then thread your rope through the halter ring and honda, as shown, and pull the slack taut.

2. To avoid a tug-of-war, you'll begin training your youngster to lead by teaching him to yield to sideways pressure on the line, rather than by pulling him forward. Sideways pressure encourages movement, as he'll have a natural tendency to yield to it with his head and neck, and/or step into it to maintain his balance. By contrast, straight-ahead pressure would cause him to instinctively brace against it. With practice, he'll translate yielding to sideways pressure to giving to the forward pressure you'll exert when you begin leading him on a straight line. He'll also learn to move forward in response to your body movements to avoid feeling pressure. (I'll demonstrate

each of the following steps on the left side. However, your youngster should learn to lead from both sides. Simply reverse your cues to perform them on the right.)

Stand about 2 feet to the side of your weanling's left hip, holding the line in your right hand and the coiled slack in the left, as shown. Gradually remove slack from the line, applying steady tension until he bends his head and neck toward you, as this filly has. Immediately reward him by releasing the pressure and praising him with kind words and rubs. If he braces against the pressure or swings his hindquarters away from it (a common response), release the pressure and slowly try again, until he accepts it and remains still. Repeat this pressure-release routine, until he'll yield to light contact.

3. Now, ask your youngster to yield while "longeing." Drive your weanling forward at a walk on a 30-foot circle by stepping toward his inside hip, as you learned in Lesson 1 (page 10). Remain 10 to 15 feet behind him, as shown. At this distance, you're out of kicking range, and he'll feel comfortable because you're not invading his "space." Allow him to walk a few revolutions without applying pressure to the line. (Notice how my rope drags the ground.) If you were to immediately remove your slack and apply pressure, you'd confuse him and he'd probably respond by pulling back, setting up a tug-of-war—the opposite of your goal.

When your youngster appears relaxed, gradually remove slack from the line, until his natural tendency is to stop because the circle is getting smaller. (This may take one or several sessions to get him to stop; keep working until he does. You may also reinforce the stop by using the verbal cue "whoa.") When he stops, immediately release the pressure, and praise him with encouraging words and rubs. Don't worry if he doesn't bend his head and neck at this point. You simply want to get him accustomed to responding to the pressure while walking. Continue this walk-stop sequence, until he quickly stops with light pressure.

Now your weanling is ready to graduate to bending his head and neck to the inside of the circle as he longes. Continue asking him to circle, gradually reeling in slack until the steady pressure causes him to bend his head and neck to the inside. His natural reaction will be to stop, rather than bend, because that's what he just learned. But now you want him to progress by maintaining his forward motion while yielding to pressure. If he stops or balks, drive him forward by looking at his hip and raising your coiled slack toward it if necessary, switching hands on the rope if you need to. (By now, your youngster should start to associate your body movements with his cues to move, so simply looking at his hip should be enough.) Repeat the last segment of this step, until he'll consistently walk a circle while bending his head and neck in response to light pressure. Then reverse these directions, and repeat Steps 2 and 3 on the opposite side.

4. Next, you'll begin decreasing the distance between you and your weanling as you longe him, gradually working your way toward the correct shoulder-to-shoulder leading position. As he continues to circle at a walk, gradually remove slack from the line until you're positioned parallel to his barrel, as shown. In this position, you're better able to drive him forward if he balks. Ideally, he'll yield to the increased pressure by bending to the inside of the circle. But he may resist the increased pressure and your close presence at first by raising his head and stiffening his neck, as this filly has. If he does, maintain steady line pressure, and continue circling until he relaxes his muscles and yields to it. Then reward him by immediately releasing the pressure and praising him. Repeat this step, until he'll circle and bend consistently with little or no pressure, in the side by side leading position. When he does, you're ready to advance to Step 6. However, if at any point he responds to the pressure by stopping...

5. ...avoid pulling on the line and dragging him. Instead, drive your youngster forward by looking at his inside hip, or by switching your hands on the rope and raising your coiled slack toward that hip if necessary, as shown. If he continues to balk, you may be progressing too fast. You'll need to drive him forward, lengthening your slack, until you're walking behind him as you were in Step 3. Then, when he's relaxed again, work your way back up to walking beside his barrel.

6. Your weanling is now ready to lead from a shoulder-to-shoulder position. From this position, he'll continue to fine-tune his ability to interpret your body movements as cues to move with you. Continue asking him to circle at a walk, gradually removing slack until your shoulder is even with his—the position I'm approaching. As in the previous steps, he should yield to the increased pressure by bending his head and neck. This filly objects to the pressure and my encroaching presence, as her elevated head and stiff neck indicate. If your youngster responds in a similar manner, keep steady pressure on the line, and con-

tinue asking him to maintain his motion until he yields to the pressure, at which point you should release the tension and praise him. If he stops in response to the pressure, refer to Step 5. When he'll consistently lead and bend in the shoulder-to-shoulder position with little or no line pressure...

7. ...guide him around a section of the circle, then on a straight line. To introduce forward pressure, walk toward your weanling's nose or step ahead of it. By now, he knows how to yield to pressure and should take a step in response to it. He's also learned to follow your body movements, so he should step forward when you do. When he does, reward him by releasing the pressure on the line and encouraging him with kind words and rubs. If he balks, avoid dragging him or jerking the line. This aggressive approach will cause him to resist pressure, and could teach him to pull back while standing tied. Instead, maintain steady forward pressure on the line, as shown, until he steps forward. Then release the pressure and reward him. Repeat this pressure-step-release maneuver, gradually increasing the number of steps he takes on a straight line, until you can guide him on a straight path with little or no pressure on the line, while remaining even with his shoulder.

8. A relaxed appearance and light contact reveal that this filly is following my body language as I lead her on a straight track. When your youngster can perform this entire lesson at a walk, repeat it in the other direction, if you haven't already. Then try it at a trot. Finally, attach a lead rope, unfasten your line, and lead him. He should respond to the pressure in the same manner. If he doesn't, return to leading him with the lariat or longe line. Eventually, begin leading him in new surroundings to further hone his skills and build his confidence.

HIND-LEG HANDLING

Teach your weanling to tolerate sensations on and around his hind legs—without fear or a fight—using this rope-work lesson.

In this lesson, you'll build on the sacking-out and leading basics of Lesson 2 and Lesson 4, respectively, by teaching your youngster to accept rope pressure around his hind legs, without kicking or panicking. By teaching him to tolerate hind-leg stimuli, you'll reap four primary benefits: 1) You'll reduce the risk of getting kicked when you handle his hind feet; 2) you'll accustom him to having a rope dangling around his legs, so he won't panic when you pull a hose around them for bathing in the next lesson (see "Lesson 6: Bathing" on page 30); 3) he'll learn to remain calm, even when entangled in the rope, helping to prevent him from getting seriously injured if he ever gets caught in a fence; and 4) you'll introduce him to having a rope dragging behind him, preparing him for future ground-driving or roping work.

You'll first sack out your weanling with the lariat. When he accepts its touch, you'll longe him, introducing him to the feel of a rope bumping his hind legs. When he tolerates that, you'll work up to wrapping the rope around his body, dropping the free end, and allowing him to calmly walk out of the entanglement.

You'll need:
• A well-fitting halter.
• A soft, cotton lead rope.
• A soft, 24- to 30-foot lariat.

1. Halter your youngster, lead him into the round pen, and close the gate. Remove your lead rope, then attach a lariat to his halter (see page 22). When he's settled, use the gradual process outlined in Lesson 2 (page 15) to sack him out with the lariat's coiled slack, which will reintroduce him to its feel. Begin by sacking out his entire front end, and gradually work your way to his back. (If you were to rub his muzzle, then go immediately to a hind leg, he might panic and try to kick or run away.)

2. When your youngster is comfortable with having the coiled lariat rubbed on both sides of his front end and back, gently touch it to his upper hind leg. To begin, stand on his left side, facing him, with the coiled slack in your right hand. Position yourself opposite his muzzle, then bend at the waist until you can touch his left hind leg with the rope, keeping your head away from his hind leg. Rest your left hand and elbow on his withers to support yourself. This position will not only keep you out of kicking range, it'll also enable you to push away if he suddenly lunges forward.

Your weanling is likely to react to the "tickling" sensation by cocking his hind leg, as this filly has. That doesn't necessarily mean he's about to kick (if he's calm and the rest of his body is relaxed), so avoid reacting by scolding him or by suddenly jerking away. You want to avoid confusing or frightening him. Instead, reassure him that he's responding correctly by returning to rubbing his head before he has a chance to kick. Then gradually work all the way down his hind leg in the same manner. Next, move to his right side, and repeat this process on that hind leg.

3. Progress by asking your youngster to accept the rope bumping his hind leg while being longed at a walk. This step gradually introduces him to hind-leg invasions while he's moving—and positions you away from his kicking gear. Drive him forward on a 30-foot circle to the right by stepping toward his inside (right) hip. Keep slack in the line, as shown, so you're not applying constant pressure on his head. (Constant pressure could cause

him to feel trapped, resulting in him kicking or running away.) Stay 10 to 15 feet behind him, and lightly bump the rope against his upper inside (in this case, right) hind leg. (*Safety tip:* If your youngster panics and tries to run away from the pressure, let go of the rope. Continuing to hold it could seriously injure both of you.)

Because you've gradually worked up to this step, your weanling should be used to the rope, so won't kick out. If he does kick, spend more time on Step 2. If he becomes nervous and speeds up in response to the rope's contact, apply light pressure to his halter to slow him down. If he tries to run off, release the line to avoid more panic, which would put you both at risk for injury. When he's settled, ask him to turn and face you, then slowly begin again. Once he "tells" you he's accepting the bumping sensation on the right side, as this filly has with her relaxed appearance and attitude, longe him in the other direction, and repeat on his opposite hind leg.

4. Next, return to longeing your youngster on a circle to the right. This time, however, reposition the rope so it's on his left side, as shown. Exert more pressure and raise the rope by reeling in slack, until you're standing about 7 feet to the side of his right hip. You're now applying constant pressure, both at the halter and hind leg, so he should respond by turning his head toward the fence, swinging his hindquarters to the

right, and reversing his direction. If he doesn't, continue taking up slack, creating additional pressure until he does. When he reverses, continue to stand at least 7 feet from his hind end, so you don't get kicked. This filly is responding to the increased pressure by cocking her leg, which is natural. But she's also remaining calm and relaxed, so I'll continue. If your weanling tenses up, go back to Step 3 and start over. Once he'll consistently yield to the pressure and reverse, praise him. At this point, he's ready to repeat the process on the opposite side.

5. Now, stand next to your youngster and wrap the line around his body, teaching him to accept increased rope pressure around his hindquarters. This exercise also familiarizes him with the sensation of the "butt strap" you may use to secure him in a trailer or washrack. Starting on his right side, slowly walk around him, wrapping the line around his hindquarters. If he appears comfortable with the rope, walk within inches of his hind legs as you step around him. (You should actually brush your weanling's hind legs as you pass by.) That way, if he decides to kick you'll just get a shove from his hocks. If he shows signs that a kick is eminent (a raised head and neck, stiff body, or a raised hind leg), stay about 7 feet away from his hind end to be safe. As you come around his left side and begin tightening the pressure on the rope, stand slightly in front of his front legs, as shown, to avoid being kicked if he reacts to the pressure. If he kicks, return to Step 4, then advance slowly. If he tries to lunge forward,

let go of the rope, then go back to Step 4 and progress slowly. When his appearance resembles this filly's (she's not cocking her foot or showing signs of nervousness)...

6. ...wrap another loop around his body, further increasing the pressure. If your youngster becomes nervous once you've completed the second loop, allow him to stand for a few minutes to relax. If he's still nervous, undo the rope and repeat Steps 5 and 6.

7. Once you've entangled your weanling in the rope, and he seems comfortable with it, let go of the free end. Then kiss to him and begin walking away, signaling him to follow you. If you've performed this lesson correctly, he should remain calm as he works his way out of the entanglement. If he panics or kicks, you've progressed too fast. You'll need return to Step 4 and slowly try again. Once he's learned to tolerate rope pressure—rather than fight it or kick—you've successfully completed this lesson.

BATHING

You want to bathe your youngster—but without a water fight. My no-stress bathing technique will teach him to stand still and relax while you spray him with a hose and shampoo/condition him.

You'll first introduce your weanling to the sight and sound of dripping water. When he accepts that, you'll increase the water pressure and mist his feet. Once he literally gets his feet wet, you'll advance to spraying his front legs, shoulders, neck, head, and eventually his hindquarters. Next, you'll shampoo and condition him, rinsing him off using the same gradual approach.

Before you begin, review these tips, as well as the "Safety Guidelines" on page 6, to help ensure your bathing sessions are safe, successful, and stress-free for you and your youngster.

• *Check your thermometer.* Bathe your youngster only on warm days (60 degrees Fahrenheit or warmer), so he doesn't get chilled. Plus, on a warm day the water will cool him, giving him a pleasant association with bathing.

• *Stay out of kicking range.* When working around your weanling's hind legs, either remain about 10 to 12 feet away from them, or stay close enough that your legs are a few inches from his. That way, if he decides to kick, he either won't be able to reach you, or his hocks will only shove you.

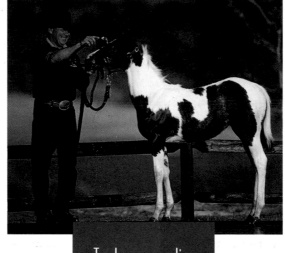

Teach your weanling the basics of bathing with this step-by-step lesson plan.

You'll need:

• An open area or an enclosure that's at least 30 feet in diameter, free of obstacles, and with no-slip footing, such as dirt, grass, or sand. You can also use a wash-rack. If you choose the latter, avoid tying your youngster, as he hasn't yet been exposed to that type of restraint. Tying him might also make him feel entrapped, possibly causing him to pull back—a dangerous habit. (*Note:* Because this filly is advanced, I'm demonstrating this lesson on an asphalt surface. Avoid such slick footing until your youngster is experienced.)

• A hose.

• A hose attachment that adjusts water pressure (optional; not pictured).

• Your favorite grooming products. (I use Absorbine Frequent Use shampoo and conditioner, because it has a pleasant fragrance and produces a silky-soft coat. Johnson & Johnson's No-More-Tears Baby Shampoo is also good for washing your weanling's face—if you accidentally get shampoo in his eyes it won't sting.)

• A rubber grooming mitt.

• A well-fitting halter.

• A soft, cotton lead rope.

1. Outfit your youngster in a halter and lead rope, lead him to your bathing area, and close the gate (if applicable). When he's settled, introduce him to the sight and sound of dripping water by turning on your spigot (or adjusting your hose attachment) just enough that water drips from the hose. Because this is his first bath, you'll gradually expose him to higher water pressure, so you avoid scaring him.

Hold your weanling with one hand and the hose with the other. Stand slightly to the side of him, with the hose slack pushed aside, as shown. That way, you won't get struck if he lunges forward, and you won't trip over the hose. Also, hold the hose several inches away from him, so he can see the water but won't be touched by it. Spraying him this early in the lesson could make him nervous and fearful of water. As water drips from the hose, gradually move it closer to him, until he relaxes and appears comfortable. He's likely to respond to the new stimuli by focusing his attention on it and flicking his ears forward, as this filly has. If he tenses up or steps away, however, avoid punishing him by jerking the lead rope and yelling "whoa." Instead, use light lead-rope pressure to guide him back to the area, then try again. It's okay if he moves around a bit. With repetition, he'll learn to accept the dripping water and not step away from it.

2. When your youngster accepts the lightly dripping water, increase the pressure and repeat Step 1, until he's comfortable with the flowing water splashing on the ground. Now you're ready to spray him, using a gradual technique similar to the sacking-out method you learned in Lesson 2 (page 15). (*Tip:* If your hose doesn't have a spray attachment, place your thumb over the opening to get a misting effect.)

Continue to stand at your weanling's side. Begin misting one of his front feet. You'll start here because it's the least likely spot to cause a spook response. When he's comfortable with that, gradually work up his leg, as shown. Each time he accepts the spray on a different area, return to his foot. This is now his comfort zone. By returning to it, you tell him he's responding correctly. If he becomes nervous, return to Step 1 or reduce the water pressure. Then slowly try again. If he steps away, use lead-rope pressure to maneuver him back.

3. As your youngster accepts spraying on his leg, slowly work up to misting his shoulder and neck in the same manner. This filly has responded to having her shoulder misted by taking a few steps, which is a common, acceptable reaction. Her relaxed body language tells me she's not fearful, so I'll use light lead-rope pressure to prevent her from moving too far. If she were to tense up, I'd decrease the water pressure or return to spraying a spot in her comfort zone. With practice, she'll learn to remain still.

4. Now reduce the water pressure again and mist your weanling's head, being careful not to spray inside his nostrils or ears. If you were to spray his nostrils, it could cause discomfort; spraying his ears could damage his sensitive inner-ear structures. Either mistake may prompt him to distrust you and the bathing process. Instead, allow water to run down his forehead. This filly's tense neck mus-

cles indicate she's nervous. My goal is to keep her relaxed, so I've reduced the water pressure even further. As she accepts the drizzling water, I'll return to spraying her feet, then gradually increase the pressure on her head. If your youngster refuses water on his head, return to sacking out his head, as you did in Lesson 2 (page 15).

5. When you can spray your weanling's head without him becoming nervous or moving away, continue to stand to the side, and extend your spray along his barrel, back, and hindquarters, using the same gradual method. As you do so, the hose may touch his legs. That's okay; it shouldn't make him nervous because you've successfully completed the rope work in the previous lesson. If it does, turn off the water and lead him away from the hose's slack. You'll need to review Lesson 5 (page 26) before you can expect him to complete this step. When you've successfully rinsed one entire side, repeat Steps 1 through 5 on the other side.

6. You're now ready to shampoo your youngster. First, turn off the water and set the hose aside. Holding your weanling with one hand, place your rubber grooming mitt on the other. I use a mitt to scrub my horses—rather than my hand or a sponge—because the massaging motion feels good to them, helping them to relax. Squirt a liberal amount of shampoo on your mitt and begin with one of your weanling's legs, gradually working up. Gently massage the shampoo into his leg, shoulder, and neck. You've successfully completed the sacking-out routine, so this shouldn't make him nervous. If it does, return to a comfort-zone area, then slowly progress.

When you're ready to scrub your weanling's head, rinse the soap off your mitt and squirt a dime-size amount of baby shampoo on it. Gently scrub his head, keeping the shampoo away from his eyes as best you can. (Even though it wouldn't sting, he still wouldn't like it.) In the next lesson, you'll clip him, so be sure to rub both ears (without soap, because you want to avoid getting rinse water in his ears), as shown, to accustom him to having his ears handled. He may raise his head and neck at first, as this filly has. But if he has a relaxed demeanor, continue to gently rub his ears. If he's quite nervous, you may be progressing too fast; in that case, back up to the previous step, and slowly start again.

When you've scrubbed your youngster's entire head...

7. ...work your way around his hindquarters, then repeat on the other side. If you walk around your weanling's hind end, position yourself out of kicking range, using the safety tip at the beginning of this exercise. (This filly has stepped away from my bathing area, so I've circled her around with lead-rope pressure, which explains her change of direction.) When you've lathered his entire body, pick up the hose once again...

8. ...and slowly rinse him off, starting at his feet and working your way up and back. After you've rinsed your youngster thoroughly, repeat Steps 6 through 8 to apply conditioner.

CLIPPING

Introduce your weanling to clippers—and the clipping process—with this stress-free method.

Now that you've bathed your youngster, you're ready to introduce him to clippers and the clipping process. Using my simple, step-by-step approach, which focuses on the head and ears, you'll teach him to accept clipping without raising his head as an evasion. You'll also teach him to do so without restraint.

You'll rub your hands on your weanling's muzzle, around his eyes, on his poll, along his ears, and on his fetlocks—the areas you're going to clip—as you did to sack him out in Lesson 2 (page 15). Then you'll blow and make a buzzing noise in his ears, simulating the sensation and sound he'll experience when you clip him. Next, you'll sack out the to-be-clipped areas with several objects to reinforce his confidence. Then you'll rub clip-

pers over the same areas, first turned off and then turned on. Finally, when he accepts the electrified clippers, you'll begin the actual clipping process.

The following tips, as well as the "Safety Guidelines" on page 6, will help make your clipping sessions safe, successful, and stress-free for you and your youngster.

• *Avoid tying your weanling.* He hasn't learned this advanced form of restraint so could seriously injure himself if he were to pull back. He'd also learn to pull back in response to scary stimuli—the opposite of your goal. Also, avoid having another person hold him. Having more than one handler could confuse him. Your goal is to teach him to accept clipping without restraint, as I'll demonstrate in parts of this lesson. If you've successfully completed each installment in this series so far, he should remain calm and still as you work around him (even without a halter). If he doesn't, halter him and use light lead-rope pressure until he does so.

• *Avoid over-clipping.* This lesson is designed to introduce your youngster to the sensation of being clipped, so limit your clipping time to 30 minutes or less, and clip only enough hair to build his confidence. As he accepts it, gradually increase the duration of your sessions and the amount of hair clipped.

You'll need:

• An open area, or a round pen or similar enclosure that's at least 50 feet in diameter, and free of obstacles. (*Note:* If you're going to try halter-free handling, perform this lesson in an enclosure in case your weanling gets away from you.)

• A well-fitting halter.

• A soft, cotton lead rope.

• At least 30 different items for sacking out (for examples, see Lesson 2 on page 15). Before you begin, arrange the items from the least frightening (such as a cotton ball) to the most intimidating (such as a plastic grocery bag and clippers).

• An extension cord (if necessary to reach your electrical outlet).

• Clippers. (I recommend using quiet clippers that don't vibrate excessively, such as Wahl's ProSeries KM-1.)

1. Outfit your weanling in a halter and lead rope, lead him to your work area, and close the gate (if applicable). If you're going to use halter-free handling, remove the halter and lead rope. Ask him to turn and face you. You're ready to rub his head and ears with your hands. Standing on his right side, gently rub his muzzle with both hands, using quick, smooth strokes. If he appears nervous, remove your hands before he raises his head or moves away, then try again. That way, he won't associate these undesirable reactions with pressure removal. Gradually rub his muzzle for several seconds, rewarding him by removing your hands and telling him "good boy" as he tolerates it.

When your youngster will allow you to rub his muzzle for several seconds, repeat the process on his poll, ears, and fetlocks. After you rub a new body part, return to his muzzle. This reinforces his positive response, building his confidence. Initially, he may raise his head when you rub his ears. If he does, return to rubbing a spot in his comfort zone, then slowly advance once more. It may take several repetitions before he accepts your ear rubbing. Here's the kind of acceptance you want: This filly is so relaxed as I rub her ears that she's laying her head on my shoulder.

2. When your weanling responds in a similar manner, extend one arm under his chin and rest your hand on the far side of his face to gently brace his head, as shown. Then lightly blow in his ear, as I'm demonstrating. The air movement mimics what he'll feel when you clip him. As before, he may react to the new sensation by raising his head. If he does, return to rubbing his ears. Then blow more gently, gradually increasing the intensity. As he accepts the blowing, reward him.

Next, make a buzzing noise in your youngster's ear, similar to the clippers' sound. Don't worry if he raises his head. Return to blowing in his ear until he appears confident, then try again. As always, reward him when he tolerates the stimuli, as this filly has (indicated by her relaxed demeanor). Once your weanling has accepted both new sensations in one ear, move to the other side, and repeat in the other ear.

3. Now sack out the areas you're going to clip with your collection of items (inset), as you did in Lesson 2 (page 15). Begin with the least-threatening object and work up to the clippers, paying particular attention to your youngster's ears. This is a review, so you shouldn't need to spend but a few seconds on each item. Take as much time as necessary, however, to ensure he's completely comfortable

with each item. (*Note:* I'm working in an open area, where this filly could easily get loose, so I placed a halter and lead rope on her. That way, I can guide her back to my area if she tries to move away.) If your weanling raises his head or becomes nervous as you rub an object on his ears, as this youngster has (indicated by her wide eyes), avoid jerking on the lead rope. Such an aggressive approach could cause him to panic and become head-shy. Build his confidence by sacking out an area within his comfort zone, then slowly try again. When he lowers his head and relaxes, reward him.

4. At the end of your sacking-out routine, introduce the clippers. Your weanling has successfully completed the previous steps and isn't afraid of having his ears handled or the sound of the clippers, so this should be easy. Gently rub the turned-off clippers over the areas you'll be clipping. Begin at his muzzle, as shown, then rub under his chin, around his eyes, and up his forehead. Work in a gradual manner, returning to his muzzle after you rub a new area to reassure him that the clippers aren't going to harm him.

5. When your weanling quietly accepts rubbing on his muzzle and face, progress to touching his poll and ears, then work down his front and hind legs. If he becomes nervous, try to remove the clippers before he reacts. Then return to an area where he's comfortable with the clippers' presence, and slowly begin again. When you can rub all of the areas without him tensing up, turn on the clippers, and repeat the above sequence.

In the beginning, hold them away from your youngster, so he can listen to the sound. Then gradually move them closer until they're touching him. This filly readily accepted the turned-on clippers, so I've taken off her halter and will finish the lesson without it. The clippers' tickling sensation may cause him to raise his head or step away. If it does, gently guide him back into position, and slowly try again.

6. If you're using halter-free handling, gently hold your weanling's head by grasping under his chin, as shown. (If you think your youngster may try to get away from you, keep his halter on or do the rest of this lesson in an enclosed area.) Then begin to slowly clip the long hairs on his muzzle in an upward motion. Clip for a few seconds, remove the clippers, then clip for a second or 2 longer. If he tries to move away, avoid holding him around the neck or he might feel trapped and panic. Instead, let him go, ask him to turn and face you, then slowly begin again. After you've trimmed a few

hairs off his muzzle, clip the long hairs under his chin. Work up to his eye hairs, using the same clip-and-remove approach. (*Tip:* Occasionally touch the clipper blades to make sure they're not getting hot. You want to avoid having hot metal burn your weanling.)

7. Next, use the same technique to trim your youngster's bridle path. Clip from mane to poll—against the lay of hair—stopping just before you reach the spot between his ears. Don't worry if you can't trim all the hair. Just trim enough to accustom him to the sensation. As he increasingly accepts the clipping process, you can get a closer trim.

When your weanling will stand quietly while you trim his bridle path, clip his ears. If he's not comfortable with this, continue clipping within his comfort zone until he's ready for you to progress. To clip his ears, gently hold one ear with your hand and trim along the outside edge in a smooth, upward motion—against the lay of

hair. Avoid squeezing his ear—you want to avoid causing him discomfort at this early stage of his training. If he moves his head away, avoid pulling on his ear. Instead, push his head toward you by applying pressure to his outside jawbone (or the lead rope if you're using one). As he tolerates ear clipping, begin trimming inner-ear hairs, if you plan to show him. It may take several sessions before you can do this.

8. Next, clip your youngster's fetlocks. (*Note:* This is optional until after you learn how to pick up his feet. See Chapter 15 on page 72) Stand opposite his shoulder, facing his hind end. Slowly run your hand down the back of his front leg, then grasp around his ankle and slightly raise his foot. If he tries to pull his leg away, gently let go of it. Then rub down his front leg and try again. If he tries to walk away, put a halter and lead rope on him. That will enable you to use lead-rope pressure to restrain him. When he'll stand quietly as you hold up his leg, place the clippers against the fetlock of the raised leg and trim upward, against the lay of hair, as shown. You can see this filly appears comfortable with the clippers because she's nibbling grass—a sign of relaxation. When you see a similar response, repeat this procedure on your youngster's other three feet. With repetition, he should allow you to clip more hair for a longer duration, without any apprehension.

SPOT CONTROL

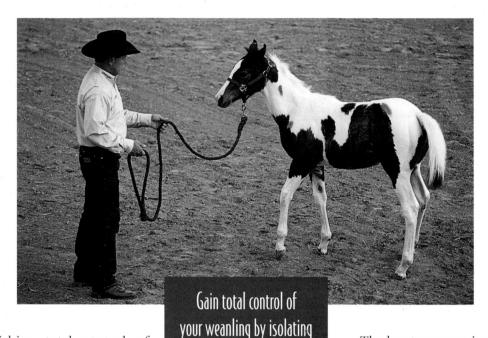

Establishing total control of your youngster is the most important aspect of his training. Before you can do so, you must first learn to isolate and control individual parts of his body. That's what I'll show you in this lesson. It's an element that's often overlooked, resulting in a frustrating, destructive relationship where the youngster—rather than you—becomes the controlling partner. You haven't communicated your boundaries or expectations, so he learns he can do what he wants, when he wants.

Before you begin, use a livestock paint stick to mark tennis-ball-sized spots on five parts of your weanling's body: the tops of his ears, each side of his muzzle and neck, and on his shoulders and hips. You'll focus on these areas to control him whenever you work with him.

Gain total control of your weanling by isolating and maneuvering individual body parts, using this simple pressure-release exercise.

The key to success in this exercise is keeping it simple. You'll make each spot—thus the corresponding body part—move with what I call a "motivator." (In this exercise, the motivator is lead-rope pressure.) First, you'll select a spot, then you'll decide where you want it to move. You'll experiment with upward, downward, left, right, forward, and backward pressure until the spot moves in each of the directions you've asked it to. As you do this, you'll notice how moving that particular spot affects placement of the others. By recognizing the connection between the parts, you'll soon be able to effectively control your youngster's movement.

To illustrate, I'm going to work from front to back, on the left side, demonstrating the pressure-release sequence in one direction. You can start with any spot, though, because you'll use the same pressure-release process for all of them. To maximize this exercise's effectiveness, however, move each spot in multiple directions, then repeat on the other side. (*Note:* If you consistently practice this lesson, you'll be amazed at how responsive your weanling will be to rein pressure when you begin his under-saddle training. That's because the pressure-release cues you'll teach him are the same ones you'll use when you ride him.)

Tip: Once you've selected a spot, avoid even thinking about focusing on another one until you're ready to progress, which is after your horse has given you the appropriate response. If you do, your body position will automatically change—so subtly that you may not even realize it—and that will change your cues, ultimately confusing your weanling.

You'll need:
• A well-fitting halter.
• A soft, cotton lead rope.
• A bright-colored livestock paint stick. (Available for less than $2 at farm-and-ranch supply stores.)

1. Outfit your weanling in a halter and lead rope, lead him to your work area, close the gate, and mark the spots. I already mentioned that lead-rope pressure is the motivator, so you're ready to select a spot. I'm working front to back, so I'll begin with the left spot on this filly's muzzle by moving it to the left. Cue your youngster to do this by standing on his left side and applying steady, lateral lead-rope pressure in the direction you want the spot to move (left). It's important that you also focus your gaze on the spot, so you avoid becoming distracted and thinking about another spot.

When your weanling makes the slightest effort to move his muzzle leftward, immediately release the pressure and praise him. He may not respond correctly the first time—he may raise or lower his muzzle instead. If he does, continue applying steady pressure until he moves his muzzle—and the spot—in the direction you've asked. Also, notice that by guiding this spot, you're also moving the ear and neck spots in the same direction. (The same principle is at work in suppling and lateral maneuvers.) When you move this spot to the left, you also cause the hips to swing in the opposite direction. That means you can control his hips by moving his muzzle. I'm going to move on, but you should stay with that and subsequent spots, experimenting with other directions.

2. Next, lower the left ear spot. Standing on your youngster's left side, apply steady, downward pressure until he starts to lower his head. When he does, release the pressure and reward him. Then repeat the sequence, encouraging him to move the ear spot lower each time, until his muzzle touches the ground. Obviously, you'll use the same cue to lower his right ear, neck, and muzzle. (This is the cue you'll use to get him to lower his head, should he raise it when you clip or bridle him.)

Here's the lightness you're after: I reach for the lead rope and this filly lowers her head, anticipating the pressure. You may wonder why I'm having you learn to control the ear spot when you can get the same results by moving your weanling's neck and muzzle spots. The reason is, when you graduate to riding your young horse, ear spots will be most visible from the saddle. When he raises his head, you'll use this cue to lower it, using his ears as your guide.

3. Use the same approach on the left neck spot. Move it backward by applying pressure until your weanling takes a step in that direction. This filly's raised neck, stiff body, and firmly planted legs indicate apprehension. (Compare her stiff position here to her relaxed appearance in Photo 2.) Her body is so stiff she can't move easily. To understand this concept, stand up and tense your entire body, especially your leg muscles. Then try to extend your right leg back. It's almost impossible. Now relax your muscles and try it. Feel the difference?

As long as this filly doesn't get overly anxious and start to pull away, I'll maintain the pressure until she relaxes and takes a step. Then I'll release it, reward her, and try again until she'll back in response to feather-light cues. If your youngster becomes fearful and tries to escape, go back to working with a comfort-zone spot, then slowly progress. When he consistently moves his neck (along with all the spots) backwards, you'll have taught your weanling to back without a lot of stress.

4. Next, proceed to the spot on your youngster's left shoulder. Move the spot to his right by facing his shoulder, using lateral lead-rope pressure, and stepping toward him. Release the pressure when he takes steps rightward, as this filly has. Repeat the pressure-release sequence until he takes several steps to the right. When the shoulder spot moves laterally, so do the other front-end spots. As he becomes more responsive to your cues and takes several sideways steps, you'll have taught him the basics of a turn on the haunches.

5. Now try moving the left hip spot to the right. Cue your weanling by applying lateral lead-rope pressure in the opposite direction you want the hip to move. For example, to swing his left hip to the right, apply pressure to the left, as shown. This will help stabilize his forehand so his hindquarters will maneuver around it. Step toward his left hip to encourage him to move it rightward. Note how this maneuver causes his hindquarters to step around his front end. At the same time, you're also moving his muzzle, ear, and neck spots leftward. This is the basis of a forehand turn.

Once you've worked all the spots on both sides of your youngster's body, and he'll move in response to light lead-rope pressure, try piecing together an advanced ground-work maneuver based on what you've learned. For example, move the ear spot forward and the neck and hip spots to the right by simultaneously applying forward and rightward lead-rope pressure. The movement should resemble a *two-track* (a forward-and-lateral maneuver in which your weanling moves diagonally across your work area) to the right. The number of combinations is endless. The more you experiment with this exercise, the more prepared your weanling will be for future lessons and under-saddle training.

WESN LESSON

Build on your foundation of control with this effective longeing lesson.

You've begun establishing total control of your weanling's movement by isolating and maneuvering individual body parts. You'll build on that foundation by teaching him my WESN (west, east, south, north) Lesson. In this exercise, you'll ask him to move in the four compass directions by circling to the left and right, turning and changing directions, and moving forward and backward in response to light lead-rope or longe-line pressure. You'll also reinforce the stop cue you learned in Lesson 4 (page 21).

Before you begin, use a livestock paint stick to mark spots on each side of your weanling's muzzle and on his hips, as you did in Lesson 8 (page 40). These are the two areas you'll use to maneuver him: You'll use the hip spots for forward motion and the muzzle spots for backward motion and the stop.

You'll first ask your youngster to walk—then trot—on longe-type circles to the left and right. Then you'll refine the skills learned in Lessons 1 (page 10) and 8 by teaching him to stop, look at you, and change direction on cue. As he becomes proficient at these longeing basics, you'll ask him to change direction more frequently, until he's changing about every half-circle. Then you'll use a pressure-release sequence to get him to back up and come to you at the walk and trot. With repetition, he'll learn to perform these maneuvers with little or no contact, keeping him light.

You'll need:

• A well-fitting halter.

• An 8- to 10-foot soft, cotton lead rope or a longe line. (I'm using a lead rope because it's easier to lengthen and shorten without excess slack.)

• A bright-colored livestock paint stick.

• A dressage whip (optional).

1. Outfit your weanling in a halter and lead rope (or longe line), lead him to the center of your work area, close the gate, and mark your spots. I'll explain how to drive your youngster on a circle to the left; reverse your cues for one to the right. Face his left shoulder at a three-quarters angle to his body. Hold the lead rope in your left hand, with its free end in your right one. This filly is responsive to light cues, so I'm allowing several inches of slack in my rope. If you need more control, hold the rope about 2 inches from the snap, and ask your weanling to walk on small circles (inset). (If you'll be using a dressage whip to encourage your youngster to move, loosely wrap the lead rope's free end around his neck so it's out of the way; hold the whip in your right hand.)

Cue your weanling to move on the circle by slowly stepping toward his inside (left) hip, gently bumping the rope's end against his hip, if necessary, as shown. (You can also reinforce your go-forward cue by clucking to your youngster.) If he doesn't move, grasp the rope closer to the snap and send him on a small circle by gently tapping his hip with your lead rope or a dressage whip (inset). As he begins to move, discontinue your bumping/tapping, gradually letting out lead-rope slack so you avoid inadvertently applying pressure, which could confuse him.

Your weanling may tense up and trot off, as this filly has (inset). If he does, slow his motion by applying light lead-rope pressure and softly telling him to "slow down" or "walk," until he does so. If he trots but remains quiet and relaxed, that's okay.

2. When your youngster circles consistently (it should only take two to four revolutions), ask him to stop. Place both hands on the lead rope and apply as much steady pressure as necessary to halt him while saying "whoa." (It's a good idea to reinforce the idea that "whoa" means stop for future under-saddle work, so always use the verbal cue.) If he doesn't stop, simultaneously apply pressure, step toward his muzzle spot to create a barrier, and say "whoa" with more authority. When he stops, reward him, allow him a moment to rest, then drive him on another circle in the same direction. (Your weanling may resist the pressure by raising his head and neck, as this filly has. With practice, he'll learn to yield to it.)

Repeat this circle-stop sequence until your youngster responds correctly with light contact. Then repeat the maneuver at the trot. When he's consistently trotting and "whoa-ing" to the left, reverse these cues for a circle to the right, then repeat Steps 1 and 2.

3. Once your weanling consistently performs the circle-stop exercise in both directions at the walk and trot, ask him to bend his neck toward the inside of the circle and look at you with both eyes when he stops. This not only puts him in position to change direction, it also keeps his attention focused on you instead of outside distractions. Guide him on a circle at a walk or trot, then ask him to stop with lead-rope pressure and your voice command.

Continue applying lateral pressure until your youngster bends his neck toward the inside of the circle. Release the pressure and reward him. Repeat this circle-stop-bend maneuver, asking him to bend more each time, until he looks at you with both eyes with little or no contact. Then repeat on a circle in the opposite direction.

4. Your weanling is now ready to learn to change direction smoothly on cue. (I'll demonstrate a change of direction from a circle to the right to a circle to the left; reverse your cues for a change in the opposite direction.) Drive him on a circle to the right at a walk or trot. When he's completed two circles, apply light pressure on the lead rope, as shown, asking him to slow his gait (not stop—you want to avoid losing forward momentum), bend his neck to the inside of the circle, and look at you.

5. Simultaneously apply upward and leftward pressure on the lead rope and walk toward your youngster's left hip (what will be his inside hip), signaling him to turn toward the inside of the circle. Swing your rope end toward his hip, if necessary, to drive him on a circle to the left, as shown. If he braces against the pressure (it'll feel as though he's leaning on the rope), use hard, steady pressure to turn him. Avoid jerking the rope, or you may upset him, causing him to rear or pull away—the opposite of what you want in this lesson. With practice he'll become more responsive. Allow him to circle two revolutions to the left or until he's calm. Then...

6. ...ask him to switch direction for a circle to the right: Apply upward and rightward pressure on the lead rope, signaling your weanling to turn, and walk toward his right hip to send him on the circle. Continue asking him to change direction every two or three circles, until he learns to relax his neck muscles and turn his head slightly toward you, putting slack in the rope and making the change on light contact. Next, gradually begin asking him to change direction more frequently. Start changing after every revolution, working to every half-circle, as he consistently responds to light contact.

7. Now, fine-tune your youngster's back-up response. In the previous lesson, you introduced him to backing, so this should be familiar to him. Here, you'll encourage him to relax his neck muscles, tuck his head so it's perpendicular to the ground, and take several smooth backward steps. This is key: He must learn to respond to pressure—not just your body language in preparation for future under-saddle work when you'll ask him to yield to the bit. Once he associates lead-rope pressure with backing, he'll be more likely to understand that backward rein pressure means "back up," too.

Stand on your weanling's left side, opposite his head. Face his hind end, holding your left hand a couple of inches from the lead-rope snap, and your right hand on the rope's free end. Simultaneously apply down-and-back lead-rope pressure and step forward, toward him. If he takes a back-up step that's great—he's responsive to your body language and pressure cues. Release the pressure and reward him. If he doesn't move, apply steady down-and-back pressure on the lead rope until he takes a step. When he makes an effort to step backward, reward him. Then continue the pressure-release procedure until he takes several back-up steps with light contact. This filly appears relaxed (indicated by her natural neck carriage). With practice, she'll learn to relax even more and "give" her head. As your youngster does, gradually ask him to take more—and faster—steps.

8. Finish this lesson by asking your weanling to come to you in response to light lead-rope pressure. This teaches him to come to you on command—the foundation for the next lesson, in which you'll teach him to do so without lead-rope pressure. That way, you'll never have to chase him around his pasture or paddock to catch him. Step about 3 feet in front of him. Apply steady pressure on the lead rope, as shown. If he resists the pressure by raising his head and neck, as this filly has...

9. ...drive him forward on a circle using the cueing sequence you learned in Step 1. Avoid tugging on the lead rope or trying to pull your youngster to you. That will only teach him to brace against pressure by pulling back—the opposite of your goal. Once he's circled a couple of times, ask him to stop as outlined in Steps 2 and 3. Then try your come-to-me cue again.

10. With practice, your weanling will walk to you—without pressure, as this filly has—as soon as you step in front of him. When he does, try this maneuver at a trot: Drive him on a circle at a trot. Then signal him to trot to you by stepping in front of him and applying light lead-rope pressure, if necessary, until he understands your cues at the faster gait.

COME ON CUE

Take the fuss out of catching your weanling—and earn his respect—with this advanced exercise.

Do you have to chase your youngster around his pasture or paddock whenever you want to catch him? If so, you probably haven't yet earned his respect or gained total control of him. Here's how to reprogram his "catch me if you can" behavior and teach him to come to you on cue.

You'll combine the cues you taught your weanling in Lessons 1 and 9 (pages 10 and 44, respectively), asking him to walk on a circle, stop, and turn to face you head on. When he consistently does this, you'll ask him to turn more frequently, then step toward you. With repetition, he'll walk to you on cue.

Review the longeing skills you taught your youngster in the previous lesson. However, for this session, perform them without a lead rope or longe line, using the techniques outlined in Lesson 1. When he consistently responds to your go-forward, stop, look-at-me, and switch-directions cues, you're ready to advance to this lesson.

You'll need:
- A well-fitting halter.
- A soft, cotton lead rope.
- A lariat.

1. Lead your youngster into a round pen, close the gate, and remove his halter. Ask him to walk on a circle to the left by stepping toward his inside (left) hip, as you learned in previous lessons. (Reverse your cues for a circle to the right.) As he moves around the pen, walk a smaller inner circle, with your body positioned behind his hip. That way, if he stops you can immediately drive him forward again. If he breaks into a trot, as this filly has, slow his motion by softly telling him to "slow down" or "walk." If that doesn't work, firmly step across the pen toward his nose to slow him down. (Avoid stepping directly in front of your weanling, or he may stop or try to turn.) If he stops, use your go-forward hip cue to ask him to move again. If he tries to change direction, step toward the front of his nose to block his turn. Then step toward his left hip to drive him back on the circle. (If you've successfully completed all of the lessons up to this point, your youngster should be comfortable with this maneuver. If he's not, review the previous lessons until he is.)

2. Once your weanling consistently walks around the pen, ask him to turn to the inside of your circle until he's facing you, then to stop and focus his gaze on you. (You can't expect your youngster to come to you on cue until you have his complete attention.) To do this, use a combination of cues that you used to teach him to turn and look at you (Lesson 1, page 10) and to change directions on the longe line (Lesson 9, page 44).

As your weanling circles the pen, briskly step toward a point on the fence that's about 20 feet in front of his nose, forming a barrier that will cause him to change direction. He should begin to turn before you reach the fence, as this filly has, putting you in position for him to easily turn and face you. If he doesn't, practice Lessons 1 and 9, until he does. When he reaches that point, signal him to stop by ceasing your movement and using the verbal cue "whoa." Allow him to stand a moment, with both eyes focused on you. If he becomes distracted and turns his gaze away, kiss to him and gently bump the lariat against your leg, if necessary, to regain his complete attention. If that doesn't work, take a couple of diagonal steps to the right, toward his left hip, and drive him on a circle again. Then try the circle-turn-focus-on-you routine once more, until he stands and looks at you for several moments.

3. Next, slowly step toward your youngster, rewarding him with rubs and kind words (inset). As you walk toward him, he may step forward to meet you. If he does so, praise him! The rest of the exercise will be simple, because he appears to be comfortable and focused on you, and he already understands the basics of coming to you on cue.

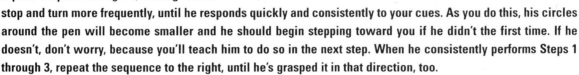

After you've praised your weanling, repeat Steps 1 through 3, asking him to stop and turn more frequently, until he responds quickly and consistently to your cues. As you do this, his circles around the pen will become smaller and he should begin stepping toward you if he didn't the first time. If he doesn't, don't worry, because you'll teach him to do so in the next step. When he consistently performs Steps 1 through 3, repeat the sequence to the right, until he's grasped it in that direction, too.

4. Now teach your youngster to walk to you on cue. Drive him on a circle to the left, then ask him to turn until he's facing you head on. This time, instead of walking to him and rewarding him, ask him to step toward you by kissing to him and bumping your lariat against your leg with increased energy. As soon as he takes a single step toward you, as this filly has, stop and reward him. Then step away from him, drive him on the circle, and repeat the entire process. As you step away, he may follow you or move off. If he does, immediately turn around, hold up your hand, and tell him "whoa" with authority. Continue the sequence, asking him to take more steps toward you each time...

5. ...until he walks within at least an arm's length of you while keeping both eyes on you. Notice how this filly's ears are pointed toward me, and her gaze is locked on me as she walks. This body language indicates I have her complete attention—thus her respect. That's your goal. If your weanling freezes up or becomes distracted and looks away, take a step to the right and use your go-forward hip cue to drive him on a circle, then try the entire sequence again.

When you can reach out and touch him, praise him. As your youngster becomes proficient at this exercise, ask him to turn and walk to you from different points and distances around the pen until he does so without hesitation. Then try it on a circle to the right.

NO-CONTACT CONTROL

In the past three lessons, you've been establishing a foundation of communication and response, leading to control of your weanling's movement. In this lesson, you'll learn how to achieve a higher level of communication and respect by leading him without a halter and lead rope.

Using a series of body-language cues, you'll teach your youngster to move beside you, stop, and back up without lead-rope contact. With repetition, you'll be able to control his movement in any direction, using

Improve your communication and control, while honing your weanling's leading skills, with this no-contact leading lesson.

just body language. That's because without headgear, your youngster can't rely on halter and lead-rope pressure for guidance. He must tune into you. Such enhanced awareness will encourage him to lead willingly, without a tug-of-war and without crowding you. *Bonus:* If his future lies in the show pen, he'll have a solid foundation for showmanship and halter.

You'll need:
• A well-fitting halter.
• A soft, cotton lead rope.
• A lariat.

1. Lead your weanling into the round pen, close the gate, and remove his halter. Ask him to walk on a circle to the left by stepping toward his inside (left) hip, raising your lariat to reinforce your go-forward message if necessary. (Reverse your cues to send your youngster on a circle to the right.) As he moves around the pen, walk a smaller inner circle, keeping your body positioned opposite his hip, as shown. If he stops, use the hip cue to send him forward again. If he begins to trot, slow his motion by saying "slow down" or "walk," stepping toward his nose to form a barrier if you need to. He should readily respond to your voice and body cues, because you've successfully completed all of the preliminary exercises. If he doesn't, practice Lesson 10 (page 49) to increase his responsiveness.

2. When your weanling consistently walks around the pen, ask him to turn to the outside of the circle, until he's facing the fence—about 90 degrees. (*Note:* You're doing the opposite of the previous lesson, in which you asked your youngster to turn toward the inside of the circle, until he was facing you.) This maneuver is the first step toward teaching him to "lead" on a circle to the right.

As your youngster moves, cue him to turn by briskly stepping toward his muzzle. In the beginning, he may try to turn toward the inside of the circle, as this filly has. To correct him, step closer to his muzzle, blocking his inward movement and signaling him to reverse direction. (Note this filly is responding by crossing her left leg over her right one to change direction. That's what you're looking for.) He may also turn 180 degrees and move to the right. If he does, stop him by saying "whoa," then step toward his muzzle, asking him to reverse direction.

When your weanling's face is perpendicular to the fence, immediately step toward his left hip, encouraging him to circle leftward again. Then repeat Steps 1 and 2, gradually asking him to turn, face the fence, and walk off more frequently, until he's doing so every one or two steps.

3. When your youngster performs the circle-turn-walk-off routine efficiently, cue him to turn toward the fence and step sideways, away from you. Teaching him to sidepass encourages him to move away from your body "pressure" and not to invade your space when you lead him.

To do so, drive your weanling on a circle to the left, then ask him to turn and face the fence. As he turns, position your body so you're also looking at the fence and standing shoulder to shoulder with him. Next, side-step toward him, leading with your right shoulder and slightly leaning toward him, as shown. He should respond by leaning right or sidepassing in that direction. When he does, stop your movement and reward him. If he doesn't move, raise your lariat until he does. If that doesn't work, nudge him to the right with pressure from your shoulder or elbow, until he moves away from you. If he tries to turn right and walk away, carefully step behind him (stay out of kicking range) and move to his right side to block movement in that direction and to ask him to reverse directions. Then return to his left side and try again.

Repeat this turn-sidepass sequence, asking your youngster to take more and more sidesteps, until he immediately steps away from your shoulder cue.

4. Next, begin teaching your weanling to follow you. From a left circle, ask him to turn and face the fence, and sidepass. Standing to his left, step backward toward his hip and kiss to him, cueing him to turn to the inside of the pen and face you, as he learned in the previous lesson. When he looks at you, ask him to step toward you by kissing to him and bumping the lariat against your leg. When he walks to you, reward him. Then repeat Steps 2 through 4, until he'll turn, face the fence, sidepass, then turn to the inside of the circle, and walk toward you without hesitation.

5. To advance, ask your youngster to sidepass on a clockwise (right) circle. This is the first phase of "leading" him on a straight line, so get into leading position with your inside (right) shoulder aligned with his muzzle. It teaches him to move his front feet, while keeping his muzzle at your shoulder—the correct leading position. With him facing the center of the pen, ask him to sidepass as you did in Step 3. This time, however, position yourself opposite his muzzle. He should sidepass on a small circle, as though he's pivoting on his hindquarters.

With practice, your weanling will begin to take fluid crossover steps, crossing his outside (left) leg over his inside one, as this filly has learned. If he shows resistance, raise your lariat. As soon as he takes a single sidestep, reward him. Then ask for more steps, gradually enlarging your circles...

6. ...until you and your youngster are walking shoulder-to-muzzle on a straight line, as shown.

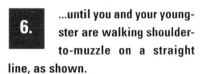

7. Next, sidepass your weanling on a counter-clockwise (left) circle, as you did in Step 5. This time, when he sidepasses, step backward so you're opposite his left hip, accustoming him to your cueing him to move forward, with all his feet, as you'll do in the next step and when you eventually lead him.

8. Next, increase the degree of difficulty by encouraging your youngster to move forward and walk beside you on a circle to the left. Position him so he's facing the center of the pen. Standing to his left, step toward his hip, using the go-forward hip cue to move him forward. As soon as he takes a step, slowly step toward his muzzle in the leading position. Slightly tip your torso forward while moving toward his muzzle, so he learns to associate your tilted position with forward movement. Any time he stops, bump the lariat against your leg and tip your torso forward to get him moving again. If necessary, drive him forward from the hip. Gradually spiral down on smaller circles. Once he reliably circles in this direction, practice guiding him left, right, and on a straight path, remaining in the correct shoulder-to-muzzle position. When you're certain you can guide him in any direction with your body language...

9. ...teach him to stop and back up in response to your body cues, rather than lead-rope pressure as you did in Lesson 9 (page 44). Position your weanling parallel to the fence, facing left. Standing about 20 feet in front of him and about 8 feet to the center of the pen. Walk toward his inside (left) shoulder. If he backs up, stop and reward him. If he doesn't, step toward his inside (left) hip and ask him to walk forward. The moment he takes a step, immediately move back to his muzzle and say "whoa" to stop him. Then walk toward his shoulder with authority, encouraging him to take at least one back-up step. As soon as he does, cease your motion and praise him. Repeat this go forward/stop/back-up sequence, until he performs it consistently.

10. Complete the exercise by turning your body around so you're facing the same direction as your youngster. Practice backing up and walking forward from this position. With repetition, he'll learn to go forward when your body leans and moves in that direction, to stop when you do, and to back up when you lean and step backward.

TIE-TRAINING

Teach your weanling to accept being tied with this yield-to-pressure method.

If you've followed my training workbook from the start, your weanling has learned the foundation skills he needs for this lesson: tying. To teach your horse to stand tied, you'll continue to hone his relax-and-give-to-pressure response, building on that response by running a lariat (and eventually a lead rope) around a fence post and teaching him to yield to its pressure—the same pressure he'll feel when tied. Once he completes my tying technique, you'll be able to tie him anywhere without him violently flailing to free himself, breaking halters and lead ropes in the process, and risking injury to you, himself, and others.

Follow these tips, as well as the "Safety Guidelines" on page 6, to help guarantee safe, successful, stress-free tie-training sessions.

• *Pick a quiet spot.* Tie your youngster in a quiet area with minimal distractions to avoid startling him.

• *Stay with your youngster.* Avoid leaving your youngster unattended during your tying sessions until he's confident, in case he pulls back or gets nervous.

You'll need:
• A well-fitting halter.
• A soft, cotton lead rope.
• A lariat.
• A solid, secure fence post. (For photographic purposes, I'm using a rail of my round pen.)

1. Outfit your weanling in a halter and lead rope, lead him to the center of your work area, and close the gate. Remove the lead rope and attach a lariat or longe line to the ring below his chin, as you did in Lesson 4 (page 21).

Reinforce the basics of restraint by asking him to yield to lateral pressure while longeing at the trot, as you did in Lessons 4 and 9 (pages 21 and 44, respectively).

Then repeat the process at a slow

lope. Adding speed will excite your youngster. If he's going to resist pressure and pull back, he'll do so at a faster gait. If he does, simply ask him to trot again by applying pressure to the lariat to slow his motion, then gradually work up to the lope. Repeat this process on a circle to the right until he delivers the desired response in that direction, too.

2. Next, encourage your youngster to yield to pressure from behind. This will reinforce the message that he must stop in response to backward pressure—a cue you'll use when you lead him to a hitching post and ask him to stop in front of it. (I'll show you how to perform this step on a circle to the right; reverse the cues for a circle to the left.)

Standing on your weanling's right side, send him on a circle to the right at a trot. As he moves, position yourself 10 to 15 feet behind him (away from his kicking gear), with your rope extended along his right side and behind him, as shown. In the beginning, he may bend his head and neck to the side slightly. If he does, that's okay; he's simply anticipating pressure.

Gradually let out slack until you reach the rope's end. Apply gentle pressure on the rope and say "whoa" to stop your youngster. Then kiss to him, asking him to yield to the pressure and turn his body to look at you. When he responds correctly, immediately release the pressure and reward him. Drive him on another circle in the same direction, repeating the process until his response is confirmed with the slightest pressure. At that point, practice the sequence at the lope, until he consistently responds to pressure at that gait. Reverse direction and practice at the trot and lope.

3. Now, ask him to bend away from you in response to pressure applied from the opposite side. It's important that he disassociates you from pressure, because when you tie him, any pressure will come from the tie post.

Turn your youngster so he's facing the center of the pen. (I'll explain how to perform this sequence from his right side; reverse the instructions to practice from the left side.) Standing opposite his right hip, out of his kicking zone, pass the rope along the left side of his neck and diagonally over his back toward his right hip, as shown. Next, apply steady pressure on the rope, until he turns his head to the left—away from you. Immediately release the pressure and reward him when he does so. Initially, he may turn toward you

as he's used to doing. If he does, move directly behind him, remembering to stay out of kicking range, and increase the pressure. As soon as he yields to it, progress by asking him to turn his entire body toward the pressure. Use the same pressure cue, except this time maintain it and kiss to him until he turns 180 degrees to the left and faces you. When he does, immediately release the pressure and reward him. Then switch sides and practice the turn-toward-pressure cue in the opposite direction.

4. Now you're ready to "tie" your weanling. Lead your youngster to your tie post, so he's standing perpendicular to it about 15 feet away. (I've worked this weanling on this exercise before, so I've positioned her closer to the fence.) Run the end of your rope around a post once (avoid wrapping it), level with his withers—the ideal tying height. (*Note:* Make sure your post is a strong, secure one—that is, cemented into the ground or firmly set.) Next, position yourself opposite

his right hip, and extend the rope over his back diagonally, as you did in Step 3. Gently apply steady pressure on the rope, until he steps toward the pressure. If he reacts to it by pulling back, immediately let go of the rope, so you avoid the risk of injuring him or yourself. Return to the previous step and slowly advance. As soon as he takes a single step, release the pressure and reward him. Repeat the process, asking him to take more steps. When he consistently steps forward in response to the slightest pressure, switch sides and perform this step in the opposite direction.

5. Next, encourage your youngster to move away from you, stop and bend toward the pressure, and step forward to relieve it. This maneuver simulates the restraint he'll feel when he's tied to a post. Position him perpendicular to the post, about 5 to 10 feet away. Stand opposite his left side and walk toward his left hip, kissing to him, to encourage him to sidestep or swing his hindquarters away from you. Run the rope around the backside of the post, and hold the coiled slack in your left hand. As he moves, let out slack, until you reach the end. Initiate your bend-toward-pressure cue, asking him to yield to the pressure and turn his head toward the post. Now, simultaneously flip the rope over his body and cross behind him to the opposite side, being sure to stay out of kicking range. (*Note:* If flipping your rope makes your weanling nervous, lead him to your round pen and take a moment to practice just that maneuver.)

Then position yourself opposite your youngster's right hip and cue him to move away from you until the pressure causes him to bend his neck and step toward the post. Continue switching sides and asking your youngster to move away from you and yield to pressure more often, until he proficiently yields to light pressure and steps toward the post.

As you work through this process, gradually take up slack, positioning your weanling closer to the post, until there's about 2 inches of slack. Practice this for several sessions, before you attempt to tie him.

6. When you can perform the side-switching sequence, without your youngster showing apprehension, tie him to the post with a lead rope. First, remove the lariat and snap a lead rope to his halter. Lead him to the post, then loosely wrap the lead rope a couple times around it (so it'll release easily if he pulls back), at eye level, giving him 5 inches of slack. Avoid leaving too much slack, as he could get his foot caught. He should be able to hold his head in a level position comfortably. If he can't, give him a little more slack.

Allow him to stand for a few seconds, then release the rope and reward him. Gradually work up to several minutes. Once he'll stand quietly and consistently, tighten the rope to 4 inches, 3 inches, etc., until he's within a couple inches of the post. When he appears comfortable, unwrap the lead rope and tie him using a quick-release knot (inset). (If you don't know how to tie such a knot, ask a knowledgeable friend to show you.) Again, allow about 5 inches of slack in the rope at first. Keep him tied in this manner for only a few seconds. Gradually work up to tying him a couple inches from the post and allowing him to stand for several minutes.

CROSSING OBSTACLES

Teach your weanling to cross three common trail obstacles with this confidence-building exercise.

Whether your eventual goal is to ride your youngster on the trail or compete in a trail class, you may need to be able to cross such obstacles as poles or logs, tarps, and bridges. Before you can expect him to negotiate these obstacles willingly under saddle, you must first build his confidence and develop his co-ordination by training him to be led across them. That's what you'll learn in this lesson. (*Note:* I'll focus on only three obstacles. But you can apply this method to any obstacle your weanling is reluctant to tackle.)

You'll begin by using the go-forward hip cue you've used throughout this train-along series to encourage your youngster to approach and walk across a series of poles—the least intimidating obstacle. Once he consistently crosses the poles without hesitation, you'll use the same gradual approach to teach him to walk across a piece of plywood and a tarp to prepare him to cross a bridge. When he willingly crosses those obstacles, you'll apply the same technique to teach him to cross a flat bridge—the most difficult of the obstacles, and one that will lay the foundation for the subsequent trailer-loading lesson.

You'll need:
- A well-fitting halter.
- A soft, cotton lead rope.
- A dressage whip.
- Four to six cones.
- Four to six poles (or 2-by-4-inch lumber).
- A 4-by-8-foot sheet of $^1/_4$-inch plywood.
- A plastic tarp (any size).
- Several heavy rocks or hay bales.
- A flat trail-class bridge. (If you don't have one, borrow or build one; some local riding arenas and trainers may keep one on hand).

1. Set four to six poles, spaced 3 feet apart, in the center of your work area. If you don't have enough poles, alternate poles and 2 by 4s, as shown. Place the cones along the right side of the poles, forming a boundary that will help encourage your youngster to walk a straight track.

Outfit your weanling in a halter and lead rope, lead him to your work area, and close the gate (if applicable). Standing a few feet in front of the first pole, with your youngster's nose pointed straight toward it, ask him to move forward toward the obstacle by initiating your go-forward hip cue: Stand on his left, opposite his shoulder, facing him. Loop the lead rope over his neck, holding it in your left hand (a couple inches from the snap) and the dressage whip in your right one. Ask your weanling to move forward by raising your whip toward his left hip, as shown, keeping his head pointed toward the obstacle with light lead-rope pressure. (Avoid pulling on the lead rope or you may cause him to resist—rather than yield to—pressure.) He should immediately respond to your cue and step forward. If he doesn't, gently tap his hip with the whip until he does. When he takes a single step, release your cue and reward him, then repeat this process.

As you approach the obstacle, your youngster may show apprehension and stop. This is the boundary of his comfort zone, where you must work on building his confidence. Allow him to stand and inspect the obstacle as long as necessary to make him feel comfortable, reassuring him with kind words and rubs. (Your weanling will probably lower his head to look at and smell it, as this filly has in Photo 4.) When he raises his head and appears relaxed, send him forward again, moving alongside him. If he balks, increase the intensity of your taps.

As your youngster crosses the obstacle, he may take a step sideways, as this filly has, to avoid having to pick up his feet and cross the poles. If he does, lead him away from them and work on controlling his various body parts, thus his straightness, focusing his attention on you by performing the WESN Lesson (page 44). Then re-approach the obstacle and try again.

2. In the beginning, your weanling may hit the poles. If he does, don't worry. With practice, he'll learn to pick up his feet, establish a steady rhythm, and take an even number of strides between the poles. Once he crosses the obstacle, walk him around it and take him over it again. When he consistently crosses the poles in that direction without hitting them, as this filly is doing, repeat the entire process from the other end.

3. Once your youngster crosses the pole obstacle from both directions without reluctance, teach him to walk across wooden obstacles. Before you begin, remove the pole obstacle, so you avoid confusing or distracting him. Set the plywood in the center of your work area. Use the same go-forward drill to encourage him to move toward it.

As you approach the wood, your weanling will probably stop and inspect it. As he does, reassure him with rubs and kind words. When he appears confident, send him forward again, clucking or kissing to him to reinforce your cue if necessary. Continue this go-forward drill, lightly tapping his hip, until he places one front foot on the plywood. When he does, reward him. If he spooks at the sound of hoof on plywood, back him off the obstacle and repeat, placing one foot on the wood until the sound doesn't bother him. Gradually repeat the process until he steps forward with the other front leg, then follows with his hind legs.

When all four feet are on the plywood, reward your youngster, and allow him to relax a moment. Then initiate your go-forward cue, asking him to walk across the wood. If he tries to step backward, intensify your taps until he steps forward. Once he's crossed the obstacle, lead him around it and try again until he walks across it without hesitation. Then repeat the sequence to teach him to cross from the other end, and then to cross its width from both directions.

4. When your weanling crosses the plywood's length and width consistently, teach him to cross a tarp. Remove the plywood; lay the tarp in the center of your work area. Anchor it to the ground with rocks or hay bales to prevent it from flapping or blowing away, which could startle him. Use the same gradual, one-foot-at-a-time, go-forward drill to encourage him to cross the tarp. When he crosses its length and width from each direction without concern...

5. ...teach him to cross a flat bridge, if you have access to one. (Initially, avoid sloped bridges, which are more difficult to negotiate.) Remove the tarp; set the bridge in the center of your work area (you may need some helpers to do so). Initiate your go-forward cue to send your youngster forward toward the obstacle. After he's inspected the bridge and appears comfortable with it, tap his hip to ask him to lift one front leg and place it on the bridge. If he tries to step back, increase the intensity of your taps until he steps on the bridge. When he does, cease your cues, and reward him. Then cue him to move forward and place his other front foot on the bridge, as this filly has. Reward him when he responds correctly. Avoid allowing him to walk forward. Instead, use the back-up cue you learned in Lesson 8 (page 40) to ask him to step off the bridge. Then repeat this entire sequence. Backing him off the bridge serves two purposes: First, it allows your youngster to practice stepping onto the bridge to ensure he's confident before crossing it, helping to assure success; second, it introduces him to the sensation of loading and unloading from a trailer, which you'll do in the next chapter. Continue this process until he steps on the bridge with both front feet without hesitation.

6. Now ask your weanling to approach and step onto the bridge with his front feet, only this time keep encouraging him to move forward, until he's standing on the bridge. When he has all four feet on the obstacle, as shown, cease your cues and reward him. Allowing him to settle a moment will help build his confidence.

7. When your youngster is relaxed, use the go-forward cue to encourage him to walk across the bridge, moving beside him as he goes.

8. My bridge's surface is narrower than the plywood. If yours is, too, your weanling may step off the obstacle with his front or hind end, as shown. Avoid panicking or scolding him, as this could teach him to fear the obstacle. Instead, ask him to slowly step off the side of the bridge. Then reapproach it and try again. This time, however, apply lead-rope pressure as necessary to keep his body straight. For example, if he tries to step off the right side of the bridge with his hind end, apply light rightward pressure on the lead rope to shift his hindquarters leftward. If he tries to

step off the right side with his front end, apply leftward pressure on the lead rope to move his front end leftward.

As you reach the end of the obstacle, your youngster may try to rush or jump off it. If you feel him try to speed up or lunge forward, apply backward pressure on the lead rope and say "easy" or "slow down" to slow his motion. Carefully lead him off the bridge and reapproach it. Repeat this process until he crosses the bridge with confidence. Then perform the entire bridge-crossing sequence from the opposite end, until he's fully confident from that direction.

TRAILER LOADING

You've established a trusting relationship with your weanling, and developed the skills necessary to communicate with him. Now, you'll teach him to enter and exit a trailer safely.

Applying the step-by-step, bridge-crossing skills learned in the last lesson, you'll ask your youngster to approach the trailer and gradually enter and exit it. Once he willingly loads and unloads, you'll accustom him to the sound and sensation of opening and closing the trailer's windows and doors, and securing the butt chain.

Before you begin, park your trailer in an enclosed area. That way, if your weanling gets away from you, he'll remain safely confined. Next, prepare your trailer. If you have a two-horse model with a side-by-side stall configuration, secure the right-hand (passenger-side) door open, keeping the left-side door closed. I prefer this method, as I can easily step backward if I need to, without running into the left-side trailer door. (If your trailer has a ramp, block the left side as much as possible by closing the top door and/or fastening the butt chain.) For a slant-load, close the forward stalls, using only the last one. If you have a stock trailer, secure the door open.

Use these guidelines, as well as the "Safety Guidelines" on page 6, to help guarantee safe, successful, stress-free trailer-training sessions for you and your youngster.

Set the stage for trouble-free trailer loading and unloading throughout your young horse's life with this proven technique.

• *Stabilize your trailer.* To prevent it from rolling, hitch it to your tow vehicle, park it on level ground, block the trailer's wheels, and apply the parking brake.

• *Avoid using force.* Avoid herding your weanling into the trailer, or using any form of pain or intimidation. These methods defeat your goal of teaching him to willingly load.

• *Avoid sedatives.* If you sedate your youngster, he may not remember the lesson, so you might have to start over next time.

• *Refrain from feeding.* Avoid bribing your weanling into the trailer with feed. Doing so not only distracts him, but also teaches him to expect a snack each time he enters the trailer. Also, if he doesn't load, you're actually rewarding bad behavior.

• *Be patient.* To avoid having to hurry through the exercise—which often results in frustration and injury—plan to devote at least 3 hours to your first loading lesson. Or do it in stages, if your time is limited.

You'll need:
• A well-fitting halter.
• A soft, cotton lead rope.
• A dressage whip.
• A trailer that has a sturdy floor (preferably covered with rubber mats to reduce slippage) and is free of sharp protrusions.
• A tow vehicle.

1. Outfit your weanling in a halter and lead rope, and lead him to your work area (close the gate if applicable). Loop the lead rope's free end around his neck, as shown, so he doesn't step on it. Standing on his left side, opposite his shoulder and facing him, grasp the lead rope in your left hand, about an inch or two from the snap, and the dressage whip in your right. Using the go-forward hip cue you've applied throughout this series, ask him to trot on a circle to the right. This maneuver not only takes away some of his excess energy, it also focuses his attention on you and reinforces the message that he must move forward in response to your cue. After he has consistently trotted a few circles to the right, ask him to reverse direction and trot on a left-hand circle.

2. Once your youngster readily responds to your cues, introduce him to the trailer. Stand him about 20 feet from the rear of your rig, with his nose pointed straight ahead. Lead him toward the trailer until he stops or shows apprehension. This defines the limit of his comfort zone, and is the point where you'll begin building his confidence.

To approach the trailer, stand on your weanling's left side, opposite his shoulder, facing him. Keep the lead rope looped around his neck, holding it about 1 to 2 inches from the snap, and grasping the whip in your right hand. Encourage him to step forward by raising your whip toward his left hip, keeping his head pointed toward the trailer, as shown. If he resists your request or tries to back up, increase the intensity of your cue by tapping his hip with the whip. If he still doesn't respond, gradually increase the taps' frequency and firmness until he moves forward. When he takes a single step, release your cue and reward him with soothing words, rubs, and a moment of rest. Repeat the step-forward sequence until he's standing directly outside the trailer's right stall.

3. When your youngster reaches the stall, offer him reassurance and allow him to relax and inspect the trailer, until he appears comfortable with its presence. As he lowers his head to look at and smell the trailer's floor, as this filly has, reward him. This indicates he's thinking about entering the stall. If he turns his head away from the trailer (a sign of resistance), use light lead-rope pressure to redirect his nose toward it. As soon as he raises his head and displays confidence, ask him to step forward again, until his legs are positioned at a distance that will enable him to easily lift one leg and place it inside the trailer.

4. Next, encourage your weanling to step forward with his hind legs, which will eventually cause him to lift one front foot and set it on the trailer's floorboard. To accomplish this, ask him to move forward, firmly tapping his hip if he doesn't respond, until he shifts his weight onto one hind leg, freeing up the other one. When he does, discontinue your tapping, and reward him. Then begin tapping his hip again, reinforcing the cue with a kissing or clucking noise as necessary, until he steps forward with his free hind leg. When he does, cease your tapping and assure him that he's responded correctly.

Repeat the tapping technique, until your youngster has both hind legs tucked under his body. This position is uncomfortable, as it places most of his weight on his hindquarter muscles. To ease his discomfort, he'll want to distribute some weight onto his front end—ideally by lifting a single front foot into the trailer. If he tries an evasive maneuver such as backing up, tap his hip firmly to correct him and send him forward. When he places a front foot inside the trailer, cease your cue and reward him. Don't worry if he paws the floor—it's a good introduction to the sound of hoofbeats on floorboards (as were the plywood and bridge phases of the previous lesson).

Once your weanling's foot has touched the trailer's floor, he may pick it up and try to back out. Anticipate his movement, so you can cue him to back up and exit the trailer before he starts moving backward. This allows him to experience unloading, and lets him know he's not trapped. Perform the step-up-back-out sequence several times, encouraging him to rest a single front foot in the trailer for a moment longer each repetition by using light lead-rope pressure to keep his nose pointed forward. When he places his front foot in the trailer and rests it there for 1 minute without hesitation...

5. ...ask him to place both front feet on the trailer's floorboard. Repeat Step 4. Once your youngster places one front foot in the trailer, continue tapping his hip until he picks up his other front foot and places it in, too. When he's standing with both front feet inside, as shown, ask him to back out. Repeat the step-up-back-out process, encouraging him to stand with both front feet in the trailer for a longer duration, until he rests them on the floorboard for 1 minute without apprehension. When he does...

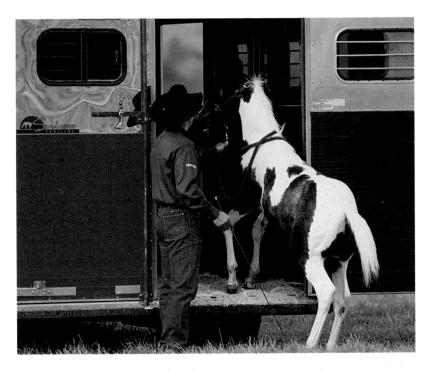

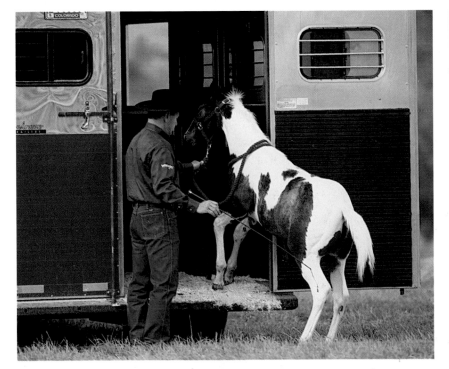

6. ...ask him to place both front feet and one hind foot inside. (Notice how I'm tapping this filly's left hind leg, encouraging her to lift it up and set it inside the trailer.)

Once your weanling has set three feet on the trailer's floor, release your cue and ask him to back out. Repeat this step, gradually asking him to rest three feet inside the trailer for several seconds, building to a point at which he'll stand for 1 minute, relaxed and confident.

7. Next, teach your youngster to completely enter the trailer. Extend the lead rope's tail across his back, so you can reach it once he loads. Ask him to place three feet in the trailer. Continue tapping for forward motion until he places his fourth foot on the floorboard. When he responds correctly, reward him. Then apply backward pressure on the lead rope's end, asking him to back out. (Never enter the stall with your weanling, as this can create a dangerous situation.) Continue asking him to load and unload, encouraging him to remain inside for a longer duration each time.

When your youngster remains quiet inside the trailer for several minutes, accustom him to trailer noises (not shown). Open and close windows, close

feed doors, swing the butt chain, etc., until these common noises don't bother him. Then secure the butt chain and allow him to stand several moments until he appears comfortable. Progress by opening and closing the door, gradually keeping it closed for several minutes until he's confident.

Next, back or lead your youngster out of the trailer, and repeat on the left side of the trailer. Loading your horse in the left side of the trailer helps keep the trailer balanced when hauling a single horse.

Once you've completed this work, you're ready to take your weanling for a ride around your farm (that is, inside the trailer). Select good, even-surfaced roads, and make starts, stops, and turns as smoothly as possible to avoid bouncing him around and throwing him off-balance, which would frighten him. Remove his lead rope and avoid tying him, so he can use his neck for balance and won't feel restricted. At first, haul your youngster only a few yards to accustom him to the trailer's movement. Then stop and unload him as a reward. With practice, you'll work up to hauling him longer distances.

If you feel him moving a little while you're driving, don't worry. The motion should soon relax him. If it doesn't, or he becomes overly nervous while you're driving—you'll feel him moving nonstop inside the trailer—immediately stop and let him settle, then proceed more slowly. Practice the entire loading and unloading process again, until he's once again confident inside the trailer. Make short hauls around the farm until he remains quiet and steady. Avoid hauling him off your farm until he's completely confident with the trailer's movement.

THE YEARLING YEAR

HOOF HANDLING

Hone your young horse's foot-handling response—without fear or a struggle—using this gradual approach.

By now, your youngster should be well on his way to becoming a solid, trustworthy partner. He's also probably approaching his yearling year, or has already turned 1. Ideally, it's best to continue to hone his skills as a yearling, rather than ignoring him until he's ready to be ridden. (Doing the latter allows the skills you've worked so hard to develop to grow stale.) The remaining six ground-work lessons are great for weanlings and yearlings alike. In this installment, you'll teach your young horse to lift his feet and accept your hold on them—a necessary skill for hoof cleaning and farrier work. (*Note:* I'll demonstrate the remaining lessons on Quarter Horse colt, Star Potential, also known as Alex.)

You'll gradually ask your yearling to move away from pressure, shifting his weight onto the opposite limb and cocking the foot you're after.

As he understands this concept, you'll sack him out with your hand, reintroducing him to the sensation of having his leg and foot touched, as he did in Lesson 2 (see page 15). Once he's comfortable with that, you'll condition him to lift his foot on cue, enabling you to easily—and safely—grasp and hold it. With repetition, he'll learn to shift his weight onto his opposite limb, lift his foot, and hand it to you without a hassle.

Before you begin, review the "Safety Guidelines" on page 6, to help make your hoof-handling sessions as safe and successful as possible.

You'll need:
• A well-fitting halter.
• A soft, cotton lead rope.
• A dressage whip (optional).
• A helper (optional).

1. Halter your young horse, lead him to your work area, and close the gate. Wrap the lead rope's free end around his neck, as shown, so it'll be out of the way. (*Note:* I'll begin with Alex's left hind foot, because that's the side from which most horses are used to being handled, and I prefer to work back to front for this lesson (you'll see why in Step 2). When he willingly allows me to hold that foot, I'll progress to his right hind foot, eventually graduating to his front feet. If you're more comfortable starting with your youngster's front feet, rearrange my instructions, and begin with his left front foot— Steps 7 through 10. Then gradually advance to his right front foot, and finally to his back feet— Steps 1 through 6. Reverse the instructions for work on the right-side feet.)

Stand facing your youngster's left side, opposite his shoulder. Hold the lead rope in your left hand, a few inches below the snap. Using the go-forward hip cue you taught him in Lesson 1 (page 10), ask him to walk a small circle around you. Performing this simple maneuver will relax him and focus his attention on you. As soon as he's walked a few revolutions and/or appears quiet and responsive to your cues...

2. ...ask him to stop. This will encourage him to shift his body weight onto his right hind leg, and cock his opposite foot, as Alex has in this photo. In this position, you can easily pick up his foot (you won't have to lean against him to shift his weight onto the opposite limb; or resort to pinching the tendons on the back of his leg). Simultaneously say "whoa" and exert constant pressure on the lead rope, until he halts. (If your young-

ster doesn't stop immediately, review yielding to pressure, outlined in Lesson 9 on page 44.)

If you're not so fortunate, and your youngster places equal weight on his hind feet or shifts his weight onto his left hind leg (in either case that foot will be planted on the ground), teach him a cue that will encourage him to move his hips a step or two to the right, thus shifting his weight in that direction.

3. Here's your cueing sequence: Simultaneously remove some of your lead rope's slack and step toward your young horse's left hip (for encouragement, tap his left hip with a dressage whip or your hand, as I've just done). Maintain light tension on the rope to prevent him from stepping forward.

The instant he makes the weight shift (he'll lift his left heel and rest his left toe on the ground), cease your cues and reward him—even if he rests his toe only a second. Repeat the weight-shift routine until he delivers the cocked-foot response you're after whenever you cue him to move his hips to the right. With each repetition, he should increase the time he stands with his foot cocked. It may take several attempts to achieve this degree of responsiveness, so hang in there. If you find yourself getting frustrated, stop for the day or perform a maneuver you and your youngster are comfortable with, ending your training session on a positive note. Then try again later.

4. Once your young horse will consistently cock his foot on cue, ask him to do so as you sack him out with your hand. (Review Lesson 2 on page 15.) This reintroduces him to your touch, so he won't be startled when you reach for his foot.

If he puts his left foot down as you sack him out, send him on a circle and repeat the stop-and-shift sequence until he lifts his heel and rests his left hind toe on the ground. When

you reach his hind leg, position yourself opposite his midsection and lean over, keeping your head to the side of his hind leg—rather than in front of it—to avoid getting kicked.

5. Gently rub your hand down his leg. When you reach your youngster's fetlock, gently press your left hand against the back of his fetlock to encourage him to bend it and lift his foot in response to your touch. Then continue by rubbing to his hoof. If he lifts his foot, gently grasp the back of his fetlock and hold his foot an inch off the ground for a second. If he doesn't lift it, that's okay...

6. ...carefully grasp the back of his fetlock with your left hand, and lift his foot an inch off the ground, as shown. Hold it there for a second, then gently place it back on the ground and reward him. (Avoid dropping your youngster's foot, as it could be uncomfortable or startling, leading to resistance.) If you suspect he's about to pull his foot away (you'll feel him tense up and begin to move his leg), try to release it before he does so, then start over. That way

he won't learn the dangerous habit of snatching his foot out of your hand. Repeat this process several times, holding the foot for a moment longer and a little higher each time. Soon, he'll lift his foot in response to your touch, and allow you to hold it at various heights for several moments without hesitation. When he shows such obedience, switch sides and repeat the entire hind-foot-handling process on his opposite leg.

7. Once you can handle your young horse's hind feet, use a similar approach to pick up his front feet, beginning with his left front foot. Stand facing his left shoulder. In this position, you'll be able to easily maneuver his front end to shift his weight onto his right front leg. Plus, you'll be out of kicking range when you reach down to pick up his foot. Holding the lead rope in your left hand, a couple of inches below the snap, apply rightward pressure on the rope's snap and nudge his left shoulder. Your youngster should respond by stepping away, as Alex is about to do. If he doesn't, cue him until he does.

As soon as he makes the weight shift—and before he takes a crossover step with his left foot—discontinue your cues and reward him. (It's not natural for a horse to cock his front foot, so don't expect it. He may lift it off the ground, however—just what you're looking for.) Each time he puts equal pressure on his front legs, or shifts his weight onto the left front leg (you'll see his body square up), repeat this side-stepping process. Before long, he should stand with his weight distributed onto his right front foot for several moments, and sidestep in response to a nudge on his shoulder. Once you've accomplished this...

8. ...sack out your youngster's front end, as outlined in Lesson 2 (page 15). Each time he shifts his weight onto both of his front legs or onto the left one, ask him to sidestep until little or no weight is on the left front foot. Rub your way down his left front leg. When you reach the back of his knee...

9. ...gently press your left hand against it, encouraging him to bend it and lift his foot. Grasp the leg behind his cannon bone, just above his fetlock, with your left hand, and hold his foot an inch or so off the ground for a second. Then gently place it back on the ground.

10. Repeat this process, gradually increasing the amount of time and the height at which you hold your youngster's foot. When he willingly shifts his weight onto the opposite foot in response to light shoulder pressure, lifts his foot on cue, and allows you to hold it for several moments at whatever height you desire, introduce him to the sensation of a hoof pick and shoeing by rubbing your fingers along his frogs and tapping the hoof with your fist or a rock. Then repeat this sequence on the right front foot. With patience and practice, you'll always experience hassle-free hoof handling.

HEAD GAMES

Bitting and bridling will be a snap after you teach your yearling to drop his head and open his mouth on cue, using these methods.

In the next two lessons you'll learn a gentle, building-block method for teaching your young horse to accept the bitting and bridling process without a battle. By teaching him the foundation skills in this month's lesson, you'll make next month's bitting and bridling session stress-free. Plus, you'll enjoy hassle-free head and mouth handling for clipping, deworming, etc. *Bonus:* If your youngster steps on his reins or lead rope, he'll know to yield to pressure—rather than fight it—helping to prevent a wreck.

You'll start by gradually teaching your young horse to lower his head in response to poll pressure, using four progressive drills. You'll apply pressure using the halter and lead rope, then with your palm. Next, you'll do it by standing on the lead rope, and then by draping the lead rope behind his head and applying pressure by pulling both sides of the rope downward. These exercises will accustom him to having his head handled, so he'll be comfortable when you slip a bridle on him and a bit in his mouth.

You'll need:

• A 50- to 60-foot round pen (or similar enclosure), free of obstacles and with good footing. (*Note:* If possible, perform this exercise on dirt footing, rather than on a grass surface as shown. In a grassy area, your youngster is likely to lower his head for a bite, rather than in response to your cues.)

• A well-fitting halter.

• A soft, cotton lead rope.

1. Halter your young horse, snap the lead rope to the bottom halter ring (under his chin), lead him to your round pen, and close the gate. Teach him to yield to poll pressure using the approach that's easiest for him to understand: apply light downward pressure on the lead rope.

Stand on your youngster's left side, facing his muzzle. With the coiled lead-rope slack in your left hand, grasp the lead just below the snap with your right hand, and exert gentle downward pressure. The moment he begins to drop his head, even if it's only a slight movement, release your pressure to reward him. Follow with encouraging words and neck rubs. (*Note:* Remember to release your pressure the instant your young horse responds to your cue. Then follow up with rubs and words of praise. If you release your pressure too late, you deprive him of his reward, slowing his learning and prompting resentment.)

If your youngster raises his head in resistance, avoid jerking on the rope or increasing your pressure. Doing so could cause further defiance, leading to a tug-of-war you won't win. Instead, continue to exert the same steady pressure. (Avoid releasing your pressure, or you'd reward his resistance.) Eventually, he'll lower his head to avoid it. As he does, immediately release your pressure to reward him.

Repeat this head-down cue, asking your young horse to drop his head lower with each request, until his nose touches the ground. Encourage him to keep his head at the new level between requests, instead of raising it, to avoid getting him in the habit of jerking up his head when you remove a bridle. The key is to anticipate the moment he's going to raise his head (you'll feel him tense up). The instant you think he's going to make that move, exert light downward pressure on the lead rope, giving him a "stay down" message. Each time he drops his head a bit lower and holds it steady, offer him encouragement and give him a moment of rest (inset). Although I've released my pressure, Alex has continued to hold his head at the same spot. This tells me he's focused on my cues. When your youngster shows such commitment to your cues, and holds his nose near the ground for several moments, allow him to raise his head and rest. To cue him, apply upward pressure on the lead rope or ask him to step forward.

2. Now apply palm pressure to your young horse's poll. (You'll use this cue next month to ask him to lower his head for the bridle.) From your position in Step 1, lay your right palm between his ears, on top of his poll. Gently press down, releasing your contact and rewarding him the second he delivers the head-down response, as shown.

If your youngster braces against the pressure or slightly raises his head, maintain it until he responds correctly. If he raises his head beyond your reach, he's not ready for this maneuver; return to Step 1.

Repeat this pressure-release sequence several times, asking your youngster to drop his head a bit lower each time, and hold it there, until his nose touches the ground. If he tries to raise his head, immediately apply palm pressure, telling him to keep it down. With repetition, he'll drop his nose to the ground with the slightest palm pressure, maintaining that position for several moments.

3. Continue your yielding-to-pressure lesson by asking your young horse to give to halter and lead-rope pressure when you stand on the lead rope. This simulates the feeling your youngster will encounter if he steps on his reins or lead rope.

Remain in the same position as before, but face forward. Release most of your lead-rope slack, placing your right foot on the rope, as shown. Shift most of your weight onto the rope, making sure you can still easily slide the rope under your boot. Take up as much slack as necessary to establish light contact. If you've successfully completed the previous two pressure-release drills, your youngster should reliably drop his head in response to this maneuver—and keep it there until you tell him to do otherwise. Reinforce his willingness with rubs and an "atta boy."

If your young horse doesn't immediately drop his head, maintain steady contact until he does. If he raises his head slightly, adjust your rope slack to the point he feels light pressure. Then progress in the sequence outlined above. If he raises his head beyond your reach, repeat the previous drill until he's ready to advance to this one.

Practice this maneuver several times, taking up slack with each repetition and asking your youngster to drop his head lower, until his nose nearly touches the ground, as Alex's has here (inset). The more you practice, the lighter he'll become.

4. You're ready for the most advanced head-down cue: draping the lead rope behind your young horse's ears, similar to a set of roping reins, and applying poll pressure by simultaneously pulling on both sides of the rope.

Standing in the same position as Steps 1 and 2, run the lead rope behind your youngster's ears, near his poll. Move toward the front of his body, so you're standing slightly in front of and to the side of his muzzle. In this position, you won't be at risk of getting hit should he suddenly jerk his head upward. With your hands on both sides of the rope, simultaneously pull both downward, exerting equal pressure. When your young horse drops his head, release your pressure and let him know he's responded correctly. Repeat this maneuver, using the same gradual approach you did with the previous exercises, asking him to gradually drop his nose to the ground and hold his head at each new level for several moments.

As before, if he resists your pressure, maintain steady contact until he drops his head. If he raises his head too high, return to the previous drill and slowly work up to this one.

5. Once your youngster reliably responds to the rope-over-the-poll pressure with light contact, accustom him to the feel of the bridling process by giving him "head hugs."

From your position on your young horse's left side, drape the lead rope over his neck or over your arm, as shown, so it won't interfere with this procedure. Next, lift your right arm and place your right palm on top of his head, between his ears. Offer him encouragement by rubbing his head and telling him how good he is. If he seems relaxed, extend your left arm over his nose, below his right eye, and place your left hand on his right cheek. Gently hug his head by pulling his head toward your torso, continuing to soothe him. Bringing his head toward you in this fashion encourages him to relax his neck muscles and lower his head. Plus, this is the position you'll want him to assume during bridling. Release your pressure just before you think he may pull his head away (you'll feel him tense up and get fidgety). That way, he won't learn to associate your release with his resistance, because you released his head before he pulled it away.

If your youngster consistently pulls his head away or tries to move away from you, practice Lesson 2 (page 15), focusing on his head. When he remains quiet as you sack out his head, return to this step.

Continue this hug-and-release process several times, increasing the duration of each head hug, until your young horse allows you to hug his head for several moments without pulling away.

6. Now prepare your youngster for bitting by handling his mouth. From your left-side position, with the lead rope out of the way, rub your hands over his muzzle. As he accepts this, gently lift his lips and rub his upper gums, as shown. If he raises his head, apply the palm-on-the-poll head-down cue, gently hug his head and pull his face back toward you, and begin again. (Actually, Alex's head should be a bit lower here.)

7. When your youngster remains quiet as you rub his upper gums, encourage him to open his mouth for the bit. Ask him to drop his head by initiating the palm-on-the-poll head-down cue. Also, ask him to bring his head toward you using the following sequence: First, reach your right arm under his jaw and around the top of his muzzle. Then pull his head toward your stomach. (For photographic purposes, I wasn't able to do that here.) Once his head is in the desired position, encourage him to open his mouth by carefully slipping your left index finger into the left corner of

his mouth, across his *bars* (the open space between his front and back teeth), and gently pressing on the center of his tongue. The instant he opens his mouth, as Alex has, remove your finger and reward him.

If your youngster refuses to open his mouth, insert one additional finger into his mouth, and press on the center of his tongue. When he finally opens up, remove your fingers and reward him. Repeat this process until he immediately opens up when you touch one finger to his tongue. Once he opens his mouth, reward him for a job well done. His willingness here will make the next bitting and bridling session a breeze.

BATTLE-FREE
BITTING & BRIDLING

In the previous lesson, you taught your youngster to lower his head on cue and open his mouth in response to finger pressure on his tongue. Now, you'll apply those same cues as you introduce him to a snaffle bit and bridle.

My gentle bitting-and-bridling technique will enable you to put a headstall on your young horse and slip a bit into his mouth without discomfort or a fight. By teaching him to accept a bit and bridle now, you'll avoid such annoying—and potentially dangerous—behavioral problems as head-tossing and teeth-clenching in the future.

You'll begin by accustoming your young horse to the sensation of having a bit slipped into his mouth. You'll first make a "training bridle" with your lead rope. Then you'll practice guiding the rope "bit" between his teeth. When he calmly accepts this bit, you'll sack him out with your regular bridle, until he doesn't mind it touching his head and ears. Next, you'll ask him to lower his head and bring his face toward you in the cor-

Putting a bridle on your young horse will never be a battle with this gentle procedure.

rect bridling position. Once he assumes that position, you'll bridle him. To finish, you'll practice the four head-down drills outlined in last month's lesson, accustoming him to the feel of wearing a bridle.
You'll need:
• A good-fitting halter.
• A soft, cotton lead rope.
• A headstall with a browband. (This style is easier to pull over your youngster's ears than a one- or two-ear model.)
• Ten- to 12-foot, soft-cotton roping reins.
• A snaffle bit. (When introducing a bit to my young horses I use a full-cheek snaffle. Though excellent for training, a full-cheek isn't legal in most Western competitions, so you may opt to use a D-ring, O-ring, or egg-butt instead.)

(*Note:* Before you begin, place your bit and reins on your headstall. Then hold the bridle up to your youngster's head and adjust it so that it'll slide on easily. If in doubt, adjust it too loosely. Putting on a too-loose headstall will be less stressful to him than pulling on one that's too tight.)

1. Outfit your young horse in a halter and lead rope, lead him to your work area, and close the gate. Teach him to accept having a bit slipped into his mouth by inserting your lead rope between his teeth. (The lead rope is softer and less frightening than a bit.) This will also allow you to practice holding a bit properly and slipping it into his mouth without causing him discomfort.

Stand on your youngster's left side, opposite his head, and face him. Next, use your lead rope to make a modified "training bridle," like the one shown. Here's how: Grab the middle of your lead rope with your left hand and lift it to your horse's forehead, running it between his eyes. Next, reach between his ears with your right hand and grasp the rope at a point that keeps it fairly taut against his face. Continue holding the rope with your right hand. Form a loop larger than his muzzle with your free end, as shown. Grasp the top of the loop with your right hand. This forms the "bit." (I avoid running the rope behind a young horse's ears, because it could make him feel confined, leading to nervousness.) Next, adjust the loop by taking up or releasing slack, until it's equal in length—or slightly longer than—your headstall.

Once you've crafted your "training bridle," gently slip the "bit" section into your young horse's mouth. First, ask him to assume the bridling position you taught him last month. Apply light palm pressure to his poll with your right hand to lower his head. When his ears are level with—or below—your shoulders, extend your left arm over his nose, below his eyes, and place your left hand on his right jaw. Gently pull his head toward your midsection.

Next, cradle the "bit" portion of your loop in your left hand, and slowly raise it toward your youngster's mouth, as shown. (For how to properly cradle a bit, see Step 4.) As you lift the rope bit, slip your left index finger under his upper lip, so you can see when he opens his mouth. Insert your left thumb into the left corner of his mouth, between the bars. If you've done your homework, he should readily open his mouth when he feels the thumb pressure. If he doesn't, he's not ready to accept a bit. Return to the previous lesson.

2. The instant your young horse opens his mouth, slowly raise your right hand, raising the rope bit between his teeth until it's resting against the corners of his mouth, as shown. As you slip it in, avoid bumping it against his teeth. This is good practice: If you were to bang a metal bit against his teeth it'd be painful, and he'd soon learn to anticipate the pain—and try to avoid it—by throwing up his head or clenching his teeth when you bridle him.

If your youngster raises his head, follow it upward with your right hand to prevent the rope bit from falling out of his mouth. Apply your palm-on-the-poll pressure to encourage him to lower his head. Once he does, you may also have to pull his face toward you again to get him in the desired position.

Hold the rope bit in your young horse's mouth for a few seconds, praising him with your voice. Then remove it by reversing the sequence outlined in Step 1 and above. If you execute this procedure correctly, the rope bit should exit his mouth cleanly, without hitting his teeth.

Once your youngster releases the "bit," reward him. Repeat this bitting routine a few more times, or until he quietly accepts and releases the rope bit.

3. Now you're ready for the first phase of bridling: sacking out your young horse's head with your everyday bridle. This will accustom him to the sensation of the headstall. (For how to sack out his head, see Lesson 2 on page 15, replacing the halter with your bridle.)

When your youngster allows you to rub the bridle over his entire head without exhibiting apprehension, accustom him to the sensation of having the crownpiece pulled over his ears. Gently place the crownpiece over his right ear with your right hand, then hold it there for a moment, as shown. Then remove the bridle and reward him. Repeat this process on the same ear, until the dangling bridle doesn't bother him. Use the same sequence on the opposite ear, then both ears.

If your young horse shows hesitation, return to rubbing a spot he'll tolerate, and begin again. If he raises his head, apply palm pressure to his poll, encouraging him to lower it. Once he calmly accepts the bridle touching his entire head and dangling from each ear...

4. ...begin the bridling process. Extend your right arm between your youngster's ears and grasp the bridle's crownpiece. Hold the bit slightly below his mouth with your left hand, so you avoid inadvertently bumping it against his teeth. Cradle it using the following technique (inset): Rest your thumb on the inside of the left cheek piece, above the mouthpiece; place your index finger under the bit's jointed portion; lay your middle, fourth, and little fingers on the inside of the bit, against the right cheekpiece.

5. Now, lift the bit toward your young horse's mouth. As you do, slip your index finger under his upper lip and place your thumb in the left corner of his mouth, between the bars, as shown.

If your youngster fully comprehended last month's lesson and the first part of this one, he should willingly open his mouth. If he doesn't, return to the beginning of this exercise and begin again.

6. When your young horse parts his teeth, simultaneously lift the headstall with your right hand and guide the bit between his teeth, as shown. As soon as he feels the bit, he may raise his head or turn away from you, as Alex has here. If he does, continue to grasp the headstall and follow his head upward with your right arm, preventing the bit from falling out and/or banging his teeth. Apply poll pressure with your right forearm to lower his head. Then pull his head into the correct position and proceed.

7. Once your youngster accepts the bit, gently slip the crownpiece over his ears, one ear at a time, beginning with his right ear. Continue to hold the bit in his mouth with your right hand on the crownpiece. Gently press his ear forward with your left hand, and slip the headstall over that ear with your right hand. Next, do the same thing with his left ear, as shown.

8. Once the bridle is on your young horse, adjust the headstall on both sides, making sure the bit rests against the corners of his mouth without applying too much pressure, as indicated by no more than one lip-lifting wrinkle. Secure your throatlatch, if your bridle has one, as shown. Allow him to stand for a few minutes and mouth the bit, so he gets used to the feel and taste of it.

9. Then further accustom your youngster to wearing the bridle, and to rein pressure, by repeating all four head-down drills presented in Lesson 16 (page 78).

At the end of your bridling session, reverse the procedure outlined in Steps 4 to 8 to slip off the bridle. Avoid removing it too quickly, or you risk bumping the bit against your young horse's teeth. Instead, slowly and gently pull the crownpiece over his ears, holding the bridle steady until he opens his mouth. Gently lower the bit until it clears his teeth. Reward him for his willingness to end this session on a positive note.

GIVE *from the* GROUND

Improve your yearling's flexibility and responsiveness to rein pressure with this seven-step suppling system.

You've taught your young horse skills that will not only instill confidence in him, but also will prepare him for under-saddle work. In this section, you'll build on your riding-prep course by teaching him to relax his jaw, poll, neck, and shoulders, and *yield* (flex) in response to direct-rein pressure from the ground.

As you practice my seven-step suppling system, you'll notice an improvement in your youngster's flexibility and responsiveness. Plus, he'll learn the basics of yielding to direct-rein pressure, as well as lateral maneuvers.

You'll first ask your youngster to soften his jaw and tip his nose slightly toward you in response to light inside (*direct*) rein pressure. You'll progress to having him bend his neck and look at you when you lift your inside rein.

Then you'll apply the same principles to teach him to maintain a flexed position while walking beside you on a circle, then while longeing. When he's mastered those maneuvers, you'll work on gaining control of his shoulders, using two lateral exercises.

You'll need:

• A 45- to 60-foot round pen (or similar enclosure), free of obstacles and with good footing. (*Note:* It's best to perform this exercise on dirt footing, rather than on a grass surface, so your youngster won't be tempted to graze.)

• A correctly fitted bridle. (See Lesson 19, Step 8, page 87.)

• A smooth-mouth snaffle bit.

• Ten- to 12-foot , soft-cotton roping reins.

• A dressage whip.

1. Bridle your young horse, lead him inside your round pen, and close the gate. Teach him to yield to bit pressure by encouraging him to deliver a "baby give" when you pick up your inside rein. By "baby give," I mean a soft jaw and slightly tipped nose. (*Note:* I'll explain how to ask for a baby give to the right. Reverse these cues for one to the left.)

Stand opposite your youngster's right shoulder, facing slightly forward at a three-quarters angle to his body. Slip your reins over his head and place them just in front of his withers, adjusting them so they're evenly draped on each side of his neck.

Ask for a baby give to the right by removing the slack from your right rein. Grasp the middle of the reins with your left hand, keeping them just in front of your young horse's withers. With your right hand, slightly lift the right rein up and back, as shown, making light bit contact with the corner of his mouth. Continue applying steady pressure until he softens his jaw and tips his nose slightly toward you. You'll know he's done so when you feel a decrease in the rein's tension. The instant you feel this, release your rein pressure. Give him an "atta boy" and a rub on the neck for responding correctly.

At first, your youngster may try to evade the pressure by shaking his head or turning it in the opposite direction. Both are normal responses; your job is to stay calm and maintain contact with his mouth until he figures out that he can release the pressure by yielding to it. He may also begin to walk—that's okay, too. Move alongside him, applying steady pressure as you go, until he yields to it.

Repeat this take-release drill several times, waiting no more than 2 seconds between repetitions, until your young horse consistently and immediately tips his nose to the right each time you apply same-side rein pressure. Reverse your cues and ask for a baby give to the left.

2. Once your youngster has mastered the baby give on both sides, he's ready to deliver a "good give"—that is, to tip his nose a minimum of 4 inches to the side, while also lowering his poll to a point level with or just above his withers. To do this, he must begin yielding to pressure with other body parts (his poll and neck), giving you even more control of his body.

To ask for a good give to the right, assume your right-side position. Follow the sequence outlined in Step 1, gradually increasing your rein pressure, until your young horse offers a good give. Repeat the take-release process, gradually asking him to maintain the good give for a longer duration, and in response to lighter contact. Reward him with instant pressure release each time he achieves the level of response you're after.

When your youngster consistently delivers a good give the moment you lift your right rein—and maintains that degree of flexion for about 30 seconds—progress to asking for a "great give," the highest degree of flexion in this stand-still drill. In a great give, he'll bend his neck to a point at which he can focus both eyes on you (about 10 inches; any more your young horse might become uncomfortable, thus agitated, and begin to brace against pressure). As with the good give, follow the take-and-release process presented in Step 1, exerting even more inside rein pressure to get him to flex through his neck.

In this photo, Alex has responded to the rein pressure with a great give. Note his position: He's relaxed through his jaw, poll, and neck, and flexing around to look at me. When you get this degree of flexion from your young horse on the right side, reverse your cues and work on achieving it on his left side.

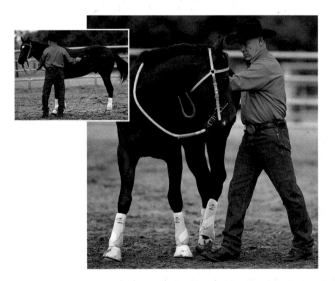

3. Now, ask your youngster to flex while walking a circle. (*Note:* In this sequence, I'll work Alex on a circle to the left. Reverse your cues for work to the right.)

Face your young horse's left shoulder, so you avoid getting kicked. Holding your left rein in your left hand, use a dressage whip in your right hand to encourage him to move forward on a small circle (about 20 feet) to the left (inset). As he moves, walk alongside him, removing the slack from your rein as you did at the standstill to encourage him to flex. This time, however, hold your dressage whip—not the center of the reins—with your other hand. The instant your young horse tips his nose the slightest bit toward the inside of your circle, release your pressure.

Initially, your youngster may tighten his neck muscles and tip his nose away from you. If he does, maintain steady pressure until he yields. If he slows his feet, as Alex has here, continue making contact with his mouth while driving him forward from the hip. Although Alex is stalling in this photo, notice how soft he is through his jaw and neck, as indicated by the bend in his neck. That's the degree of flexion you're looking for.

Repeat this circle-flex maneuver several times. With each repetition, increase your pressure, encouraging your youngster to further flex his neck and tip his nose farther toward the inside of the circle (but not so far that he loses forward motion). Ask him to hold that position for increasingly longer periods of time, until he consistently walks on a circle and maintains a bend in his neck each time you make light contact with the corner of his mouth. Reverse your cues, and practice this circle-flex exercise to the right.

4. Next, encourage your youngster to maintain his flexion as he halts, increasing his responsiveness and your control. Send him on another walk circle (as a reminder, I'm working Alex on a circle to the left), initiating your give-to-pressure cue as he moves.

When your young horse consistently maintains his flexed position for an entire revolution, ask him to stop. Maintain steady contact to keep his neck flexed, while exerting additional pressure on the inside rein to encourage him to take two crossover steps with his hind legs, as Alex is doing in this photo. As he takes these crossover steps, his hips will swing rightward, and his front legs will stop moving forward. He'll also begin pivoting on his inside front leg, eventually stopping his motion. Once he halts, drive him forward on another circle and repeat this maneuver. With repetition, your youngster will learn to immediately halt when he feels the increased exertion, and will maintain his flexion. When he does, modify your cues and use this technique to get the desired response in the opposite direction.

5. Increase the difficulty of the circle-flex maneuver outlined in Step 3 by asking your youngster to maintain his flexion as he walks a circle to the left around you. (For this drill, imagine you're longeing your youngster, but remain in one spot, rather than walking alongside him.) As with the other circle drills, drive him forward on a circle to the left, removing the slack from your inside rein to get him to give with his nose and neck.

At first, your young horse may tense his jaw and neck muscles. If he does, maintain steady contact with his mouth until he yields to the pres-

sure. If he overflexes, tipping his nose more than 10 inches (inset), he'll lose forward motion. To correct this, slide your reins forward, at least 12 inches in front of your youngster's withers. Apply rein pressure against his neck, as if you were neck reining him. Continue applying your neck-rein cue until his head and neck are straight. Then initiate your flex cue again and start over.

As soon as your young horse responds correctly, release your rein pressure. Repeat this step, asking him to yield more (but not more than 10 inches) and for a few seconds longer each time. Once you've accomplished this drill on a circle to the left, reverse your cues and repeat to the right.

6. You're ready to add lateral work, which will free up and help you gain control of your youngster's shoulders. You'll ask him to walk on a circle to the left and flex toward the inside of that circle. This time, however, you'll increase the degree of difficulty by encouraging him to take a diagonal step to the right, away from the circle, while maintaining flexion.

Here's how. Send your young horse on a circle to the left, stepping alongside him. As he moves off, lift your inside rein with your left hand to encourage him to flex. Once he does, gradually exert upward and sideways pressure on that rein, until he shifts his weight onto his right (outside) shoulder and steps diagonally to the right to regain his balance. (*Tip:* Think of it as asking him to step on the 1 o'clock mark of a clock if 12 o'clock were straight ahead.) The instant he takes a diagonal step—even if he doesn't maintain his flexion—give him a release-reward.

If your youngster tenses his body and/or doesn't step rightward, try the sequence again, exerting whatever pressure it takes to get the desired response. Then continue to refine his response with repetition. When he responds correctly without hesitation, advance by asking him to take two diagonal steps, then three, and so on. You'll soon notice him walking on a diagonal line with feather-light contact. When you see such progress, reverse your cues and work to ingrain the desired response in the opposite direction.

7. To further enhance your control, ask for bigger lateral steps. Repeat the sequence outlined in Step 6. On a circle to the left, intensify your inside rein cue to signal your young horse to step toward the 2 o'clock mark, then 3 o'clock, and so on, when working on a circle to the left. As he completes this "clock work," he'll have performed a sidepass to the right. Practice this maneuver until he consistently sidesteps rightward across your work area. Repeat the process on a circle to the right. When you've improved his forehand flexibility and increased your control over his nose, poll, neck, and shoulders, you'll be ready to take charge of his hindquarters in the next lesson.

REIN-HIP RESPONSE

In this lesson, you'll refine the forehand control, lateral work, and rein responsiveness you achieved in the previous lesson, while encouraging your youngster to move his hindquarters away from you when you deliver a rein cue. You can use this hindquarter-control exercise not only to keep from getting kicked, but also to stop him from bucking should he do so when you start riding.

You'll ask your yearling to walk on a small circle around you while maintaining his flexion

Control your youngster's hindquarters by teaching him to move his hips in response to rein pressure.

in response to rein pressure. Then you'll ask him to stop and take two crossover steps with his inside hind leg, swinging his hips away from you. When he performs this maneuver efficiently, you'll ask him to step more quickly and to take larger steps.

You'll need:
- A correctly fitted bridle.
- A smooth-mouth snaffle bit.
- Ten- to 12-foot-long, soft-cotton roping reins.
- A dressage whip.

1. Bridle your yearling, lead him to your work area, and close the gate. Ask him to walk on a circle to the left, standing opposite his left shoulder so you avoid getting kicked. Hold your left rein in your left hand, approximately 6 inches from the bit, and initiate your go-forward hip cue by stepping toward his inside (left) hip or tapping it lightly with a dressage whip. (Reverse these cues for a circle to the right.)

When your youngster has walked several revolutions without attempting to stop, ask him to flex his neck and turn his nose toward the inside of the circle. Initiate the cueing sequence you learned in the previous lesson: Slowly and gently lift your left rein slightly up and back, making light contact with the corner of his mouth. This is review, so he should readily respond by flexing his neck muscles and turning his nose toward you, as Alex has done here.

Notice how I've applied just enough pressure to encourage Alex to flex his neck 8 to 10 inches to the inside of our circle. Avoid asking for more flexion, or your youngster will become uncomfortable and agitated. Plus, doing so will teach him to brace against pressure.

2. Once your young horse maintains his flexion while walking on a circle, prepare him to take crossover steps with his hind legs—as he pivots around his front ones. Slowly and steadily increase your rein pressure to form a barrier that will prevent his front legs from moving forward. Step toward his hip to move his hindquarters, reinforcing the move-over message with a kissing or clucking noise. Maintain constant contact with his mouth until he follows up his flexion by stopping his front legs, as Alex has done here. (Notice how his hindquarters are still moving and he's beginning to pivot around his left front leg. This is the response you're after.)

If your youngster doesn't move his hips, or attempts to step forward, gradually increase your rein pressure to block him. In both cases, reinforce your move-over message with a kissing or clucking noise, raising your hand toward his left hip—or even stepping toward his hip—if necessary. (If you must do the latter, be sure to maintain your rein pressure, so he can't step forward with his front legs.)

3. Once your young horse has stopped his forward motion, avoid releasing your rein pressure. Instead, continue holding your contact until he shifts his weight onto his outside (right) hind leg, as shown. This will free up his inside (left) hind leg to take a fluid crossover step. When he makes the weight shift, maintain your rein pressure until...

4. ...he takes a step to the right with his left hind leg. If your youngster does this correctly, he should cross his left hind leg in front of his right hind, pivot on his inside front leg, and move his hips away from you. (In the beginning, he may move his right front leg forward a bit to keep his balance, as Alex has done in this photo. That's okay; with practice he'll learn to keep it stationary. If he does so on the first try, that's one thing less you'll have to work on. Be sure to reward him for his effort.)

If your youngster doesn't move his hips away from you, repeat the sequence until he does. The moment he takes a lateral hind-leg step, reward him with a rein release. Reinforce his good behavior with rubs and reassurance.

Repeat this sequence, gradually asking your young horse to take two

crossover steps. Once he performs this two-step maneuver in response to a light rein request, hone his side-stepping skills by asking him to move more quickly while taking larger steps. When you're satisfied with the results to the right, move to his left side.

FIRST SADDLING

By now, your yearling should be a trusting, tractable individual. He's also approaching his 2-year-old year, and starting to show the mental and physical maturity he needs in order to be ridden. In this lesson, you'll continue to gradually prepare him for his first ride by introducing him to the saddling process.

(*Note:* By encouraging you to saddle your yearling, I'm not telling you to ride him immediately. This is an exercise to prepare him for that event, so when the time comes, it'll go as smoothly as possible for both of you.)

First, you'll sack out your youngster with a lariat and blanket to relax him. Then you'll place a blanket on his back, and introduce him to cinch pressure by hugging him around his heartgirth. When he accepts your hugs, you'll allow him to smell and look at the saddle. Once he's comfortable with the saddle's presence, you'll place it on his back, tighten your cinches and breastcollar, then ask him to move.

Before attempting this exercise, keep these tips in mind; also review the "Safety Guidelines" on page 6.
• *Check your cinches.* Make sure your front and back cinches and breastcollar are adjusted to fit your youngster. Also, ensure there aren't any damaged or loose straps that could break or catch a hoof.
• *Recruit a helper.* I'll perform this lesson without a

Saddle your young horse for the first time without a struggle, using this force-free method.

halter or bridle. If you're not comfortable doing so, ask an experienced horseperson to hold your young horse. Be sure that individual stands on the side opposite you for safety. Avoid tying your youngster; he could panic and pull back, risking injury. That could also teach him to pull against pressure—a dangerous habit.
• *Keep him calm.* When your yearling is relaxed, he's less likely to endanger either of you and better able to focus. You'll know he's comfortable when his head, neck, and tail are in a natural position, and he has one or both ears pricked toward you. If you encounter resistance, stop what you're doing and return to a drill he's familiar with. Slowly advance as he gains confidence.

You'll need:
• A well-fitting halter.
• A soft, cotton lead rope.
• A lariat.
• A saddle pad.
• A saddle with a front cinch (and breastcollar if you'd like). (Initially, avoid introducing a back cinch, as your youngster may be sensitive to the pressure and spook. When you do add a back cinch, shorten the strap between the front and back cinches to position the back cinch farther from his flanks.)
• A helper (optional).

1. Lead your yearling into the round pen, and close the gate. Remove his halter. Begin this lesson with a simple sack-out session to relax him. (For more on sacking out, see Lesson 2 on page 15.) Stand on his left side and rub a coiled lariat on his forehead. After you've done that for a few seconds, turn and walk a few steps away from him to remove your touch. (If he follows you, that's okay; it indicates confidence and that he's focused on you.)

Repeat the rub-walk-away sequence, gradually progressing to your youngster's ears, poll, neck, shoulder, front leg, and hindquarters as he willingly allows you to brush the rope across each spot. Also, speak to him in a soothing voice for encouragement. Once you've rubbed the rope over his entire left side, repeat this step on his right side.

If your youngster becomes nervous and moves away from you, he's exhibiting signs of fear. Return to stroking an area he's comfortable with, progressing only when he's quiet.

2. When your yearling accepts the lariat, progress by sacking him out with a saddle blanket. Slowly approach him with a folded blanket, allowing him to smell and look at it. When the blanket's presence doesn't bother him (he'll look away or nibble on grass), sack him out from both sides with the blanket folded, then unfolded.

As you reach your youngster's midsection, lay the blanket over his back, sliding it back and forth along his spine, as shown, so he becomes accustomed to its feel. As he tolerates the blanket, sack him out with increased intensity, further accustoming him to the object. Wave the blanket in the air, and toss it onto his back. (Be sure not to induce any pain.) If your young horse shows apprehension, slow down and work at his pace. If he takes off, calmly approach him and slowly begin again. Be sure to stay out of your horse's kick zone while you work through this step.

3. Once you've familiarized your yearling to the blanket, introduce him to cinch pressure by hugging his heartgirth. Put the blanket on his back. Stand facing his left side, behind his shoulder. Reach your right arm over his back, just behind his withers, extending it as far down his right side as you can. Wrap your left arm under his belly, just behind his elbow, where the cinch would lie. When you're in position, squeeze his barrel and release in one quick, smooth movement. It's important to instantly release your pressure before he has a chance to react, so he doesn't learn to associate your release with any bad behavior on his part. After releasing your hug, step away to remove your touch. Repeat this hugging drill several times, gradually increasing its pressure and duration, until he stands quietly without showing displeasure.

If your youngster displays signs of crankiness, such as trying to bite you or pinning his ears, back off for a moment, then hug him again—easing your pressure. If he gets away from you, tell him to "whoa," assume your left-side position, and deliver another hug.

4. Now, introduce your yearling to the saddle. Place your saddle blanket on his back. Pick up your saddle and slowly approach him with it. Allow him to inspect it, as Alex is doing, reassuring him that it isn't a horse-eating monster. When he's no longer interested in the saddle...

5. ...move to his right side. (When saddling a young horse for the first time, I prefer to do so from the right, or *off-side*. That way, I don't have to fuss with dropping the cinches, possibly startling him.) Place your left stirrup over the horn. Slowly lift your saddle and gently set it on your yearling's back in one smooth, forthright motion. Avoid heaving it in the air or allowing it to drop on his back. Doing so could startle him, and/or cause pain and discomfort.

If you've successfully completed previous steps, the saddle shouldn't bother your youngster. (Notice how Alex is quiet and looking the other way—a sign of confidence.) If you sense he's nervous and may run off (he'll appear tense or frightened), remove the saddle before he has a chance to do so. Set it out of the way and regain his attention using the circle, stop, look-at-you exercise outlined in Lesson 1 (page 10). When he displays a relaxed demeanor, start over with Step 1, moving extra slowly through it and subsequent steps.

6. When your yearling accepts the saddle on his back, slowly move to his left side, and gently lower your left stirrup. Fasten your cinches and breastcollar, if you have one. First, fasten the front cinch. Reach under your youngster's belly, grasp the cinch, and pull it toward you. (Keep your head up, out of kicking range.) If he remains quiet, gently tighten the cinch enough to keep your saddle from slipping off when he moves, but not so much that you frighten him. Next, fasten the back cinch, if you opt to use one. Secure it so that it barely makes contact with his belly. If you make it too tight, he may buck. If it's too loose, he could get a foot caught in it.

Now, slowly bring your breastcollar around the front of your youngster's chest, and secure it in place. (Stand by your youngster's side as you do this, rather than in front of him, so he won't hit you if he suddenly lunges forward.)

7. Once you've fastened all of your straps, immediately step away from your yearling in case he explodes. (If you have a helper, have him/her unhook the lead rope and do the same.) As you move, stay focused on your horse, so you can get out of the way if he suddenly bolts. Then allow him to stand for a moment and become accustomed to it.

If he does react with fear, step toward his nose (but not in front of him where you could get run over) to ask him to change direction, then drive him forward with your hip cue. (Be careful to stay out of kicking range.) Continue to ask him to change direction and move forward until he's relaxed. Then ask him to stop and look at you. Performing this exercise takes his mind off the saddle, and soon he'll realize he has nothing to fear.

When your young horse is standing quietly, ask him to walk or jog on a circle to the left, using your go-forward hip cue, and being careful to stay out of kicking range. His first step may be a lunge, followed by a buck, as Alex is about to do here. If it is, avoid overreacting. Instead, continue to drive him forward to release any remaining bucks. As he moves, speak to him in a soothing tone to build his confidence and calm him.

8. When your yearling is relaxed and moving forward reliably, ask him to reverse direction and move on a circle to the right. Once he's moving consistently in that direction, continue to build his assurance by gradually asking for changes of direction more frequently and incorporating speed transitions. (See Lesson 9 on page 44.)

When your youngster appears comfortable moving with the saddle, as Alex is here, ask him to walk for a few minutes to cool him down. Then reverse Steps 5 and 6 to remove your saddle. Return to your yearling's left side and stand near his shoulder so you avoid getting kicked. Work slowly, keeping your movements smooth and calm to avoid spooking him. Gently lower all straps so their

swinging won't frighten him. Once you've removed the saddle, immediately step out of his way in case he scoots off. If he does the latter, allow him to calm down, then catch him and repeat the saddling process—moving even more slowly.

Congratulations—you've completed this phase of your youngster's training. ❑

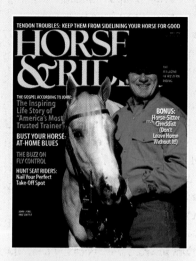